IONA

For my father-in-law, W.F. Ritchie

HISTORIC  SCOTLAND

Iona

ANNA RITCHIE

B. T. Batsford Ltd / Historic Scotland

Typeset by Bernard Cavender Design & Greenwood Graphics Publishing
and printed by The Bath Press, Bath

Published by B T Batsford Ltd
583 Fulham Road, London SW6 5BY

A CIP catalogue record for this book is
available from the British Library

ISBN 0 7134 7855 1 (cased)
      0 7134 7856 X (limp)

(*Front*) Iona
(Copyright Mick Sharp)

(*Back*) The Monymusk Reliquary
(Copyright, Trustees of the National Museums of Scotland)

Contents

Illustrations

Colour plates

(Between pages 64 and 65)

Acknowledgements

I am grateful to the series editor, David J. Breeze, both for the invitation to write this book and for his patient encouragement during the writing process. Several people were kind enough to read and comment on the text, which has benefited greatly from their help; I am much indebted to Ian Fisher, David Breeze, Anne Macaulay, Sally Foster, Richard Fawcett, W.F. Ritchie and Graham Ritchie. I should also like to thank Monica Kendall of Batsford and Pauline Marsh for their editorial help, and Alan Braby for his reconstruction drawings and maps (**3, 5, 9, 12, 16, 18, 38, 40, 66**). This book could not have been written without the inspired work on Iona of Ian Fisher and the Royal Commission on the Ancient and Historical Monuments of Scotland. I am indebted to the Royal Commission for the majority of the illustrations (Crown Copyright: **2, 7–8, 10–11, 13–15, 17, 19–24, 28–30, 33, 35–8, 42–53, 55–7, 59–61, 65, 69–71, 74, 76–91**), and also to Historic Scotland (Crown Copyright: **3, 4, 5, 9, 12, 16, 18, 27, 38, 40, 54, 62–4, 66, 72–3, 75**), to the Trustees of the National Museums of Scotland (back cover, **34, 67–8**), to Mick Sharp (front cover, **58**), to the Board of Trinity College, Dublin (**41**), to the Society of Antiquaries of Scotland (**25, 31**), to Ian G. Scott (**32**) and to Graham Ritchie (**6**, and **colour plates 1–2, 4–5, 7–9, 11–12**).

Introduction

Iona beckons, across time and nation. This small island has become an icon of Christianity and spirituality, perhaps more so in modern times than at any other period since its heyday in the sixth to eighth centuries. There may be a greater need to seek spiritual renewal now, when society has a more secular outlook than ever before. Many travellers from the seventeenth century onwards included Iona on their itinerary and recorded their impressions of the island, but few seem to have had any strong sense of pilgrimage. The basalt columns of Staffa drew them as strongly as the ruins of the medieval Abbey on Iona. It was the creation of the Iona Community in the twentieth century that led to a new phase of pilgrimage, based on George MacLeod's vision of restoring simultaneously the physical church on Iona and the spiritual passion of the Church in Scotland, thereby uniting work and worship in early Celtic tradition (**1**).

The story of Iona in recent centuries has been well told, and it is not the purpose of this book to rehearse that story. Ronald Ferguson has traced the history of the Iona Community and written a biography of the Reverend George MacLeod, and E. Mairi MacArthur has told the story of the islanders themselves (1990 and 1995), as well as collecting extracts from the accounts of early travellers to the island (1991). Iona's history has been well served by Alexander and Euphemia Ritchie (1928) and others. The present book is concerned with the archaeology of the island, both in its local context of Mull and the Inner Hebrides and, particularly in the Early Historic period, in the wider context of links with Ireland, Pictland and Northumbria. All the ancient monuments of Iona can be visited and enjoyed over just a few days, but exploring their role in the early medieval world is another matter, even if it is simply conducted from the fireside armchair. We are fortunate to have a detailed account of the visible archaeology and architecture on Iona itself in a volume of the Inventory of Argyll monuments by the Royal Commission on the Ancient and Historical Monuments of Scotland (1982). In academic terms, this was largely the work of Ian Fisher, the foremost authority on Iona's ecclesiastical buildings and sculpture.

In 1874–6, Robert Rowand Anderson took on the task of consolidating the ruins of Iona Abbey on behalf of the 8th Duke of Argyll (**2**). In 1899 the duke relinquished responsibility for the Abbey and other major buildings to the newly formed Iona Cathedral Trust, and one of the architects involved in the restoration of the church for the Trust in 1908–10 was P. MacGregor Chalmers. Once the Iona Community had been formed, there was an immediate need for accommodation for its members, and the architect Ian G. Lindsay was asked to provide designs for restoring the monastic complex round the cloister. This restoration was completed in 1965.

1 Iona Abbey today.

The medieval Benedictine Abbey that has been lovingly restored in the twentieth century was the second major building phase in the ecclesiastical history of the island. The first was the early Christian monastery founded in AD 563 by Columba, an Irish priest whose native name was Colum Cille. Columba died in Iona at the age of 75 on 9 June 597, and the story of his life and achievements was written by a later abbot of the Iona monastery, Adomnán, in the late seventh century, a mere three generations after Columba himself. Seminal translations and commentaries on Adomnán's *Life of Columba* have been published by A.O. Anderson and M.O. Anderson (1961 and 1991) and Richard Sharpe (1995). The importance of Iona to the historian and archaeologist is that, as a result of Adomnán's work, much is known about its founder, Columba, and about the monastery itself. In addition, archaeological excavations have confirmed and extended this information, particularly the work of Charles Thomas, Peter and Elizabeth Fowler, Finbar McCormick, Richard Reece, John Barber and Jerry

O'Sullivan. Although only MacLean's Cross is in the care of the Secretary of State, another ten sites are scheduled as monuments of national importance, and Historic Scotland has played a major part in recovering Iona's medieval heritage by advising and funding excavations over many years.

We know more about the physical character and everyday life of Iona than about any contemporary early medieval monastery in north Britain, and what we know is consistent with the picture obtained in Ireland. But there is also an astounding literary heritage, from Adomnán to monastic annals, illustrated gospel-books and poetry. The volume by Thomas Owen Clancy and Gilbert Márkus on the poetry of the Celtic monastery of Iona demonstrates the richness of the surviving literary tradition (1995). It is dedicated to the memory of John Smith, leader of the Labour Party in Britain, who was buried in the Abbey's cemetery in 1994, his gravestone one of the most tangible reminders of the role that Iona has played in the national consciousness of the twentieth century.

Today the island is in the care of the National Trust for Scotland as a result of the generous gift to the nation in memory of Lord Fraser of Allander of the Fraser Foundation, who bought the estate from the trustees of the Argyll Estates in 1979. The Abbey, St Oran's Chapel and the Nunnery remain in the ownership of the Iona Cathedral Trust and MacLean's Cross in the care of the Secretary of State for Scotland.

2 Iona Abbey and St Oran's Chapel before restoration; photograph by George Washington Wilson in the 1870s.

11

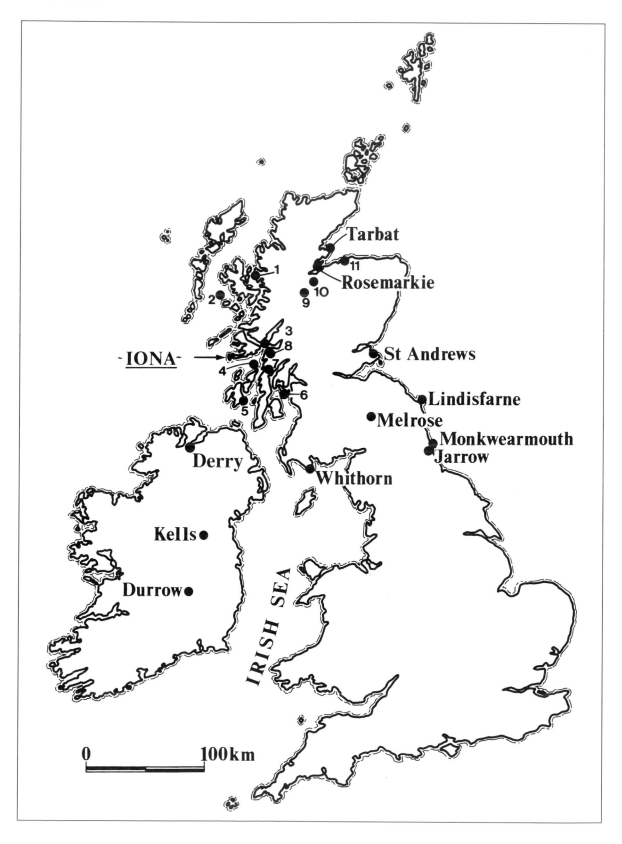

3 Map showing the location of Iona and other major early Christian monasteries and forts in Scotland, northern England and Ireland. The numbers refer to sites in western and northern Scotland: 1 Applecross, 2 Canna, 3 Lismore, 4 Eileach an Naoimh, 5 Kildalton, 6 St Blane's, 7 Dunadd, 8 Dunollie, 9 Urquhart Castle, 10 Craig Phadrig, 11 Burghead.

Justification for another book on Iona lies in an archaeological distillation and interpretation of the evidence for the island's prehistory and early history, related to the remains visible today and to contemporary remains in Mull and farther afield in Argyll. National Grid References for sites (e.g. NM 257223) are given in the section on places to explore, and, for visitors wishing to see more of Iona's antiquities than simply those around the village and the Abbey, the Ordnance Survey Landranger map sheet 48 (1:50,000) is essential. The core of this book is concerned with the character of Iona in early medieval times and with the role that its monks, particularly Columba and Adomnán, played in relation to the kingdoms of the Dál Riata, the Picts and the Northumbrians (**3**). References in the text to Adomnán's *Life of Columba* are given in the form (III, 4), i.e. Book III, chapter 4.

1
The island of Iona

In the second century AD, a Greek geographer working from Alexandria in Egypt recorded a name for the island we know as Mull. He was Claudius Ptolemaeus, and his name for Mull was Malaius. Ptolemy, as he is normally now known, derived his information from various sources, but ultimately his Latin place-names are thought to relate to the existing local Celtic names. Iona was too small to be recorded separately, and its original name is now lost. For all the beauty of the modern name, Iona, it is no more than a misreading by a scribe in late medieval times of the name used in the seventh century by Adomnán: Ioua insula. Ioua appears to have been derived as a descriptive term from an Old Irish word *eo*, meaning yew tree, and *insula* is Latin for island. Although yew is lacking from the pollen record for this period, the record is limited to the area around the Abbey and, as yet, there are no records for the previous thousand years. If, as seems likely, Adomnán's name was an Irish version of the older Celtic name, there may have been yew trees on the island in Iron Age times.

One of the various spellings of the name was I, which survives not only in the modern Gaelic name for the island, I Chaluim Chille, Iona of Colum Cille or Columba, but also in Dùn I, the hill of Iona. The Gaelic place-names of Iona are fascinating in themselves. The Iona Community has published a very useful folding map at a scale of 1:10,000 (1983), which has the names of every topographical feature both in Gaelic and in English. Many of the names are, however, of relatively recent origin.

Rocks and landscape

On the map, Iona appears to be a detached toe of the Ross of Mull, but in fact the geology of the two islands is very different (4, 5). Mull's scenery is dramatic and varied, the drama provided more than 60 million years ago by giant volcanoes. Layers of lava were laid down, 1800m (5907ft) thick, as the volcanoes erupted time and time again, and the lavas hardened into fine-grained basalts. Weathering of these horizontal basalt layers, particularly by glacial action during the Ice Ages, resulted in the stepped profile of the hills of north Mull, as well as the famous columns of the island of Staffa. The heart of all this volcanic fury lay in central Mull at the head of Loch Ba, and the collapsed and eroded crater-area has become a complicated maze of various igneous rocks beloved of geologists. This is a harsh and rugged landscape, with Ben More rising some 966m (3170ft) above sea-level. The long promontory known as the Ross of Mull runs westwards between the open sea and Loch Scridain, changing character west of Bunessan. The basalts give way first to a band of mica-schists and then to the famous red granite, and the landscape is dominated by low rounded hills and lochs. Ross of Mull granite has been exported and used in buildings thousands of miles from its source. In particular, it was used by Alan Stevenson to build the lighthouses of Skerryvore and Ardnamurchan, for which purpose quarries were opened up at Camas

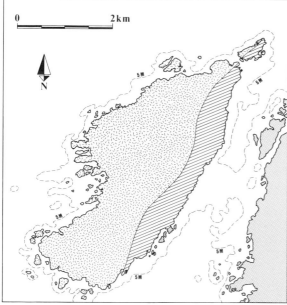

4 The rocky foreshore of St Ronan's Bay, with the village and the Abbey in the distance.

5 Geological map of Iona, showing the 5m (16.4ft) submarine contour.

Tuath on the north coast of the Ross in 1839. Traces can be seen of the railway track that carried the granite blocks to the jetty, and there are two terraced rows of quarry-workers' houses. Mull sandstone was also an important source of building stone, quarried at Carsaig Bay on the south coast. It was used from the twelfth century onwards for fine dressed masonry in the ecclesiastical buildings of Iona and Mull, and for later medieval graveslabs, although it tends to weather badly.

In contrast, Iona's bedrock is similar to that of Tiree and Coll away to the north-west rather than an extension of the Ross of Mull. There are rocky islets of red granite in the Sound of Iona, including a string along the south-east coast of Iona (Eilean Mór, Eilean Carrach, the appropriately named Sgeir Ruadh, or red rock, and the adjacent skerries), but a geological fault has ensured that the granite does not extend to Iona itself. There are, however, granite boulders on the island, transported from the Ross of Mull in Glacial times by the inexorable movement of ice. At Port na Frainge on the north-east coast there is a gigantic boulder left perched on a rocky outcrop.

The island lies on the eastern fringe of the great geological plate of Lewisian gneiss that includes Tiree, Coll and the Outer Hebrides. This is one of the oldest and hardest rocks in the world, pushed up from the lower part of the earth's crust. The western part of the surface bedrock of Iona is composed of grey gneiss, while in the eastern part the gneiss is overlain by sandstone and grits. At the south-east end of the island, a band of limestone provides the white to pale green stone known as Iona marble. One of the pleasures of visiting the beautiful St Columba's Bay is searching the beach for the small green pebbles washed up by the sea. A visitor in 1802 landed in the bay and 'picked up gray pebbles beautifully marked; fine lapis nephriticus; jaspers, green mixed with red; serpentine stone, gray and other porphyries; pure white marble and many other rare stones'. Iona pebbles, as they are known, have long played a part in the island's tourism; a record from 1806 relates that 'It is a sort of trade among the children here to collect pebbles and sell them to strangers.' Thirty-four years later, another visitor complained: 'Even before we touched land we were besieged by a troop of half-naked amphibious-looking boys, who emulously presented to our notice plateful of Iona pebbles.'

Iona marble was quarried from at least as early as the seventeenth century, and an old altar-table in the Abbey was renowned for the beauty of its white Iona marble. Unfortunately it was also known to be lucky for ships to carry a piece of that same altar-table, with the inevitable result that nothing survives. According to Dr Johnson in 1773, it was destroyed by the 'superstition of the inhabitants', who believed that 'a fragment of this stone was a defence against shipwrecks, fire and miscarriages'. In the late eighteenth century, the Argyle Marble Company was formed to extract on a commercial scale marble both from Iona and from Tiree, but it was short-lived, probably because of the problems of obtaining and transporting large blocks of the stone. The quarried band of marble is about 7m (23ft) wide and thick, and it outcrops near Rubha na Carraig Geire on the south-east coast. It is predominantly white in colour, streaked with green serpentine. What is visible of the quarry and its machinery today reflects the most recent episode of quarrying, early in the twentieth century (6). This was again a small-scale and short-lived enterprise, the Iona Marble Company.

The marble quarry is a dramatic and evocative sight, and it is easy to appreciate that exporting the blocks of marble either by sea or overland can never have been an easy task. There is a

6 The marble quarry with the cutting-machine and, beside the quarry-face, the horizontal gas engine.

narrow steep-sided gully, some 50m (164ft) long, with a mass of debris and unfinished blocks of marble at its seaward end. The remains of a gas engine and a cutting-machine still survive, the engine made in Gloucester and the cutting-machine in Arbroath; these make the quarry an unusually interesting example of industrial archaeology. The marble was quarried by blasting and the chunks were cut into rough blocks ready for export. Farther inland are the foundations of a rectangular building known as Tobhta nan sassunaich, House of the Lowlanders, which may have been used by the workforce of the Argyle Marble Company of the 1790s. Nearby are the concrete foundations of an early twentieth-century building.

Iona is a long oval island with its own offshore islets, the largest of which are Soa Island to the south-west and Eilean Annraidh to the north-east. Iona itself is 5.5km (3.4 miles) long and 1.5–2.5km (0.9–1.5 miles) wide, covering an area of about 800ha (1976 acres). The Sound of Iona, the channel separating the island from the Ross of Mull, is only about a kilometre wide, with a sandbank in the middle, and its tidal currents are fast (up to 2.5 knots) and difficult to navigate. Despite its proximity to Mull, Iona was effectively remote, simply because the crossing was not an easy undertaking. The shortest route is that taken by the modern ferry, from Fionnphort to St Ronan's Bay, but before the piers were built the regular steamboat came into the Sound from Bunessan and sent a small boat into St Ronan's Bay. Coffins destined for burial on Iona were traditionally landed at Martyrs' Bay, immediately south of St Ronan's Bay (7).

There are many other natural harbours that could be used by those approaching Iona from the open sea. A glance at any detailed map reveals how frequent all round the island are coastal names incorporating port or harbour, ranging from the substantial Port Beul Mór (Harbour of the Big Mouth) near the south-west tip to tiny Port na Frainge (French Harbour) at

7 Sketch of Martyrs' Bay in 1848–9 by Henry D. Graham; coffins arriving by sea were rested on the mound, An Eala, before being carried along the Street of the Dead to Reilig Odhráin.

the north-east. The latter has been utilized for the electric power cable from Mull, but a row of four old boat-nausts or shelters is eloquent witness to its former status as a natural harbour. The nausts appear today as long sunken rectangles end-on to the sea, and they would have been built as hollows revetted by stone walling, each with its lower end open to allow the boat to be hauled into its shelter. The west coast faces the mighty Atlantic Ocean and the prevailing westerly winds, and here sheltered harbours are more difficult to find. The evocatively named Camus Cùil an t-Saimh, the Bay at the Back of the Ocean, is mostly quite unsuitable as a landing-place, despite its large size, owing to the extensive rocky outcrops or skerries in the bay.

Some of the port-names are likely to be relatively recent coinings; Port Làraichean, for example, at the south end, means Harbour of the Ruins, and the ruins in question are of no great antiquity.

The highest point on Iona is the summit of Dùn I, only 100m (330ft) above sea-level, and most of the island is much lower, although the interior is very rugged, with rocky outcrops and peaty hollows. The sea-cliffs can be precipitous and daunting – they rise to 50m (164ft) at Druim Dhughaill on the south-east coast.

Iona was not an obvious landfall for boats sailing from the northern Irish coast, for they would naturally take the shortest crossing towards the Mull of Kintyre. The Mull itself was a hazard, with tidal races at its tip, but following its western coast into the Sound of Jura offered a sheltered route northwards. Avoiding the sometimes fearsome whirlpool in the Gulf of Corryvreckan between Jura and Scarba, travellers would pass through the Sound of Luing into the Firth of Lorn and the Sound of Mull and northwards between Coll and Ardnamurchan.

Domesticated Iona

Despite its rugged interior, there is a substantial area along the north-east coast and across the middle of the island to the machair or sandy grasslands of the Bay at the Back of the Ocean which has long sustained cereal crops and cattle (**colour plate 1**). Although this area is only about one-third of the island, it is, as James Boswell observed in 1773, 'a very fertile island and the people are industrious'. The machair is now mostly pasture, but it is still possible to see the parallel ridges left by ploughing. The main crop was a primitive form of barley known as bere, but oats and potatoes were also grown. Despite evidence for the use of small mills in the seventh and eighth centuries AD (pp. 68, 73), in the nineteenth century there was no mill in Iona and the islanders' corn was taken by sea to a mill at Bunessan in Mull to be ground. If for any reason that was impossible, they resorted to using hand-mills or querns, as had their prehistoric ancestors. The shell of the Bunessan mill still exists.

A stream passes to the immediate north of the Abbey (8). Named Sruth a' Mhuillinn (Mill Stream), it rises in Lochan Mór and runs south and then east through the monastic enclosure to the sea at Port a' Mhuilinn. Its course has been artificially improved, at least in part, on several occasions in the past. Today it is not an impressive water-course and carries little water, but its name suggests that it was once more substantial and capable of powering at least one mill. As a prelude to remedial work on the north bank, excavations were carried out by Jerry O'Sullivan in 1991 in the area to the south of Burnside Cottage. They revealed that there had once been a sub-rectangular basin and five large timber posts set into pits on the north side of the stream. The most likely interpretation of these features is that they represent the undercroft of a small mill. Water, controlled by a dam and sluices, would be directed into the undercroft, a subterranean chamber which housed the horizontal wooden paddles that drove the millstones in the upper chamber. If this was indeed the site of such a mill, known as a horizontal mill, its date is unfortunately uncertain. Its superstructure was probably

8 Iona Abbey and the village from the air.

flimsy, and it could belong to any period between the sixth century AD and the late eighteenth century, after which date we know that grain was sent to Bunessan for processing. One such horizontal mill survives in the care of Historic Scotland in Orkney, near Dounby, and several survive in Shetland, but these date from the eighteenth and nineteenth centuries, and they have survived because they were built of stone. Closer to Iona, there are traces of such a mill dating from the seventeenth or early eighteenth century at Balmavicar in Kintyre.

A visitor in 1787, James Bailey, was impressed not only by the fact that a 'large surplus of grain is annually laid up for exportation', but also by the fact that kelp had also become 'a very lucrative article as the rocks on the back of the island are peculiarly abundant in the wrack from which it is manufactured'. The 'back' of the island is its Atlantic coast, and the amount of wrack or seaweed tossed up on the shore is reflected in at least one place-name: Sloc nam Ball, or Tangles Gully, on the north-west shore (tangles is another name for seaweed). A visitor in 1788 found women burning kelp at St Columba's Bay and singing in Gaelic, 'a melancholy ditty'.

Kelp was one of the life-giving industries of the eighteenth and nineteenth centuries in Scotland. In areas such as Mull and Iona where the sea deposited large amounts of seaweed on the shore, drying and then burning the kelp brought landlords a welcome extra source of income. It was burned in shallow rectangular pits along the shore; the heat turned the seaweed into a boiling liquid, which cooled into a solid mass, when it could be broken up into lumps for transportation. Kelp was a valuable source of iodine and potassium salts and was used in the production of glass, soap and dyes. The remains of kelp-burning pits are often visible on Scottish foreshores.

Seaweed had also been used since much earlier times as fertilizer for the fields and, as a last resort, as fuel along with animal dung and turf. Iona lacked substantial deposits of peat (apart from a short period after the draining of Lochan Mór in about 1750, which provided a source of peat for about a century), but there were plentiful supplies on the Ross of Mull. Study of pollen from archaeological contexts has shown that the tree cover on Iona at the time of the foundation of Columba's monastery in the mid-sixth century AD included oak, ash, birch, willow and probably hazel. The needs of the monastic community for timber and for clearing land for cultivation and pasture had a swift effect upon the surrounding woodland, virtually eliminating oak and ash, and in subsequent centuries timber of good size had to be imported from the Ross of Mull.

2
Iona in prehistory

The end of the last Ice Age in Scotland was marked by rapidly rising temperatures, the melting of the last glaciers (including one on Mull), and a corresponding rise in sea-level caused by vast quantities of melt-water. Around 7000 years ago the sea-level was about 10m (33ft) higher than today, but in time it fell again, as the land rose, relieved of the great weight of the ice. This process has left old shorelines, known as raised beaches, as visible terraces above the present shore. There are two very distinct raised beaches along the east side of Iona, from Traigh Mór northwards, and the Abbey and village stand on the terrace between them. The higher and older beach is about 20m (66ft) above present sea-level, and the other is just above the 10m (33ft) contour and is particularly clear to north and south of Port na Frainge. It is often on these raised beaches that traces are found of the earliest inhabitants of the west of Scotland.

There were certainly people living in the Inner Hebrides from at least 7000 BC. Camp-sites dated by scientific analysis (radiocarbon dating) to the three following millennia have been excavated in the islands of Rum, Risga, Oronsay, Islay and Jura, and traces of human activity in the form of scatters of flint tools and debris from flintworking have been found in Colonsay. The life-style of hunters and gatherers leaves little physical trace, and their seasonal camp-sites are difficult to locate. As yet, in the vicinity of Iona, only one certain site has been found on the island of Ulva, off the west coast of Mull, and none in Mull itself or in Iona, but a programme of systematic fieldwalking would probably identify concentrations of flints. Occasional finds of Mesolithic artefacts have been made in sand dunes in Ardamurchan, Coll and Tiree, and a small number of worked flints have been recovered from the raised beach along the east coast of Iona and from Port na Curaich. All this adds up to a picture of regular exploitation of the natural environment of the islands by communities of Mesolithic settlers. In some cases they seem to have returned to the same place time and time again over a very long period. The camp-site on Ulva is a cave, where there is a Mesolithic rubbish heap at the entrance; it is only 8m (26ft) across, yet it is known from radiocarbon analysis to have been used over a period of some three millennia.

By about 4000 BC, an alternative life-style based on farming was known in Scotland. It was not necessarily an improvement on the old, and its adoption seems to have taken place earlier and with greater enthusiasm in some areas than in others. In Argyll, the advantages of hunting and foraging appear to have outweighed those of farming for most people until as late as the middle of the third millennium, and coastal resources of fish and shellfish remained an important element in the economy of later times. The houses of the new permanent farming settlements are likely, however, to have been built of timber and wattle, and traces of their post-holes and hearths are as difficult to locate as those of the more ephemeral shelters of Mesolithic peoples. The best indicator of the development of farming is a change from forest to open grassland and crops, and this change can only be detected from the pollen record, the study of which needs much detailed work before the vegetational history of the Inner Hebrides will be fully understood.

A tomb for Neolithic ancestors

Domestic settlements of Neolithic farming communities have been excavated in mainland Argyll and Islay, and the presence in Mull of one example of the type of burial monument used by such communities suggests that the new life-style had been adopted here, at least by some people, before 2500 BC. Their tombs were vastly more substantial than their houses and can usually be identified from surface remains. The tomb at Port Donain on the east coast of Mull has not been excavated and has been robbed of many of its stones, but it is still recognizable as a long cairn with a burial chamber at the wider northern end. The building of a tomb like this was a massive undertaking for a small community, and its achievement reflects the importance to that community of its ancestors. In the absence of written records, archaeology has little hope of assessing the ideas and beliefs of such a community, but the physical remains allow some informed guesswork based on the study of comparable but more recent peoples. Ancestor-worship is a common element in the belief-systems of primitive peoples, and ancestors are proof of a community's right to its lands – just as they are for the land-owning families of today.

Apart from this one example of a chambered tomb in Mull, there is some evidence from chance finds of artefacts of Neolithic activity in both Mull and Iona. One of the most characteristic Neolithic tools was the axe, made of polished stone and used in woodworking. Five such axes have been found in Mull and

three in Iona, but stray finds such as these can be an illusion in the sense that they are highly portable and that their final resting-place may not bear much relation to the location of their origin or working life. Stone axes seem to have been 'traded' or exchanged over wide areas. Petrological analysis of the igneous stone from which they were made can identify the source of that stone, and it is clear that suitable rocks were roughed out into axes and distributed over wide areas of the British Isles. The axes from Mull and Iona have not been subjected to petrological analysis, but it is likely that they came either from Tievebulliagh in County Antrim in Northern Ireland or from Killin in Perthshire. It is also possible that some of the Mull and Iona examples arrived at a later date. In Ireland, so many Neolithic stone axes have been found on sites of early historic date that it is thought that they may have been collected and used as smoothing irons in the preparation and care of linen clothing. They may have been used for the same purpose in western Scotland, and thus their find-spots may be far from their original homes.

Nevertheless, it is likely that there were Neolithic farming communities in Mull and Iona. From evidence elsewhere, these would be individual farmsteads with dwelling houses and outhouses for cattle and storage. The life-style of such a community depended upon a range of activities: breeding cattle, sheep and pigs, growing barley and perhaps wheat, hunting deer and seabirds and, very important, fishing in sea and loch. The potential gifts of the sea were immense, not just fish but also shellfish and the carcasses of seals and whales; the latter provided oil for lamps and bone for artefacts, furniture and roof-rafters. The tools of these people would be made of wood, bone and stone, and there would be vessels made of pottery as well as of leather, wood and stone.

A new era opens

Communal burial-places appear to have outlived their importance towards the end of the third millennium BC, and the sealing of the chamber after the last burial proved to be the end of the use of the tomb. But it was often not the end of the use of the monument as a landmark, as a link with the past or a statement of political supremacy. At Port Donain, a stone-built box or cist was inserted into the back of the cairn to take a burial of Bronze Age date. Unfortunately, nothing is known of its contents, but it is likely to have held the burial of a single individual with grave-goods and to have represented the ascendancy of a new social order.

Part of that new social order included the knowledge of metalworking, which was introduced into Britain from north-west Europe, particularly from the area around the lower reaches of the River Rhine, from about 2700 BC. The earliest metal artefacts were made of gold and copper, and they are likely to have been brought to Britain by small numbers of immigrants identifiable by their use of a new type of pottery. This is known to archaeologists as beaker pottery, tall jars that look like large drinking beakers – and in a few cases a residue inside the beaker has been analysed as the remains of an alcoholic drink made from honey and herbs. Complete beakers have been found in graves, along with metal objects and other prestigious artefacts, including archer's equipment. The individuals buried in such graves were clearly part of a new social elite, perhaps controlling access to the metalworker's skills. The greatest concentration of beaker graves in Scotland is in the East and South, but there are scattered examples in the West, including two in Mull.

As yet no beakers or bronze artefacts have been found in Iona. However, sherds of beakers found in sand-dunes in Ardnamurchan, Coll and Tiree suggest that settlement in the area may have been more intensive than the archaeological record can yet demonstrate.

Standing stones and cairns

Mull is particularly rich in standing stones, from individual stones to alignments of five, and the

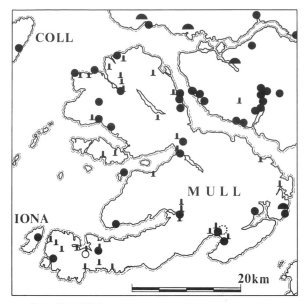

CAIRN
CHAMBERED CAIRN
BARROW
STONE CIRCLE
STANDING STONE

9 Map of early prehistoric monuments in Iona and Mull.

fine stone circle at Lochbuie (9). The study of archaeoastronomy remains controversial, but it seems certain that there was a special interest in the moon among the inhabitants of Mull four thousand years ago. There are no standing stones on Iona itself, but there are several factors that may explain this apparent lack of interest in a monument that was so popular in neighbouring Mull. Standing stones are particularly vulnerable to later use as building stone and gate-posts, and, in this holy island, such pagan relics may have been deliberately cleared away. It has been claimed that a stone circle in Iona was destroyed in AD 1560 by order of the Synod of Argyll because people continued to worship in it, but the date is too early (the first recorded synod was in 1562) and the survival of pagan customs in Iona, of all places, seems most unlikely. But there is also the geological factor: Iona's bedrocks were essentially unsuitable for tall slabs, particularly as standing stones were only very rarely

10 Blàr Buidhe kerb-cairn.

set on the hillside to the south-west of St Columba's Hotel. It is oval, almost 7m (23ft) across and only 1m (3ft) high, and it appears to have had a kerb of large boulders; only two are still in position, but five more lie close by (10). There are several such cairns in Mull, but neither these nor the Iona example have been excavated to modern standards and nothing is known of their contents. Similar cairns have, however, been examined in mainland Argyll, in Lorn and Morvern, and they enclosed deposits of cremated human bone, dated by radiocarbon analysis to the end of the second millennium BC.

These are all recognizable as burial and ritual monuments, but more difficult to interpret is the extraordinary group of cairns on the raised beach at Port an Fhir-bhréige at the south end of Iona (11). There are about fifty of them, mostly ranging in diameter from one to three metres and less than 0.5m (1ft 8in) high. Two are distinctly larger, about 6m (20ft) across and 1.6m (5ft) high, and these are each surrounded

quarried. Wooden poles, like totem poles, may have been used instead of stone, and these, of course, would survive only a few generations.

The earliest monument that has been identified in Iona is a small cairn, Blàr Buidhe,

11 Pebble cairns on the beach at Port an Fhir-bhréige.

by shallow ditches. They are all built of pebbles from the beach, and it seems unlikely that they are burial cairns. According to tradition recorded from the eighteenth century onwards, they were built as a penance by monks, but Ian Fisher has suggested that they may have been created gradually by pilgrims in medieval times.

Despite its appealing name, the cairn on the summit of Druim an Aoineidh in south-west Iona is modern. It is known as Càrn Cùil ri Eirinn, which means Cairn of [him who Turned his] Back on Ireland, and is traditionally associated with St Columba, but the tradition is first recorded in the late eighteenth century.

Just inland from the machair at the Bay at the Back of the Ocean is a natural mound known both as Cnoc an t-Sithein (Fairy Mound) and as Cnoc nan Aingeal (Hill of the Angels). The latter name arises from the traditional identification of this mound with Adomnán's account of Columba's vision of angels (III, 16). In 1774, Pennant described a cairn within a small circle of stones on top of this mound, but no other record exists of any such cairn or stones, and it may be that in retrospect he confused the site with somewhere else. Pennant also described a custom of racing horses round the mound at Michaelmas.

Later prehistory

Throughout Britain, the centuries around 1000 BC were marked by deteriorating weather. Many upland areas became unsuitable for settlement, as the formation of peat accelerated, and competition increased for the remaining good farmland. An overt element of aggression in society can be seen both in the output of the bronze industry and in new forms of settlement. The production of weapons such as spearheads and swords began to outstrip that of the farmer's axe, and communities found the need to defend themselves and their belongings within fortified enclosures. Mull and Iona were not exempt from these social changes.

There is one fort in Iona and no fewer than fifty-two forts and two brochs in Mull, mostly concentrated on the Ross of Mull and in north Mull and predominantly close to the coast (**12**). There has been so little excavation that the chronological sequence of these fortifications is still unclear, but they are likely to span the centuries between the middle of the first millennium BC and the early centuries AD. The forts are mostly small in size with strong stone walls, and they are normally built in locations of natural defence, such as rocky promontories, hilltops or small islets, and there are often outer lines of walling across the approach to the fort. The larger forts enclosed houses, but the very small ones were in effect fortified houses, where the entire structure could be roofed over, and brochs can be seen as taller and stronger versions of such massive roundhouses. Brochs are more common farther north, but two have been identified on Mull (at Ardnacross and Dun nan Gall), one on Lismore and two on Tiree. They are circular, with a very thick wall and relatively small internal diameter; there are galleries, cells and stairs within the wall, and they were multi-storeyed. There was clearly a flourishing population in Mull during the latter part of the first millennium BC, and the two brochs may represent the strongholds of paramount warlords

12 Map of forts in Mull and Iona.

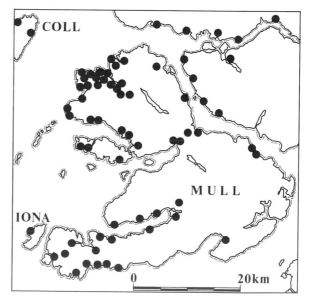

13 Dùn Bhuirg on its rocky hilltop.

of the turn of the millennium. In terms of the available good agricultural land, it is entirely appropriate that Iona should have had just one fort. As elsewhere, there would have been a peasant population living in more ephemeral houses and providing the inhabitants of the fort with food supplies. Iona's fort has become known to archaeologists as Dùn Cùl Bhuirg, but its proper name is simply Dùn Bhuirg, Hill of the Fort (Cùl Bhuirg means Back of the Fort, as in the farm-name and Gleann Cùl Bhuirg). It lies on a prominent craggy hill at the north end of the Bay at the Back of the Ocean, commanding wide views over the west coast and the machair, the island's prime agricultural land and therefore the greatest source of wealth (**colour plate 2**).

The hill possesses good natural defence, and access is not easy (**13**). The summit is only about 45 by 35m (148 by 115ft), and rocky outcrops reduce the area suitable for occupation; the community living here can never have been large, perhaps no more than the family and warrior companions of Iona's Iron Age chieftain. The seaward flanks of the hill are very steep and needed no defence, but there are the remains of a stone wall enclosing the eastern half of the summit (**14**). It is best preserved on the south side, where the outer face of the wall can be seen and where the wall survives to a height of one metre (3ft 3in). The entrance was probably on the north-east side, where access up the hill is easiest, but there is no surface trace of the gateway. Excavations were carried out between 1957 and 1959 by Peter J. Fowler, as part of an Iona research programme directed by Charles Thomas on behalf of the Russell Trust (**15**), and a small trench was dug in 1968 by Richard Reece specifically to obtain a sample of animal bone. The excavations were concentrated in the eastern part of the fort, where traces of occupation were most likely to have survived, but a small flat terrace at the south-west corner was also explored. Structural traces were disappointingly few but were compensated by an extraordinary amount of broken pottery. A small cairn of stones in the south-east part of the fort is modern, and it is this sort of activity that may account for the

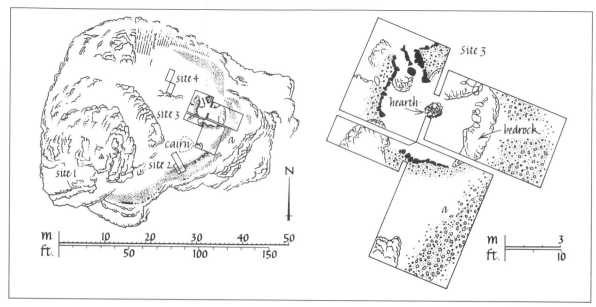

14 Plan of the fort of Dùn Bhuirg.

poor preservation of the fort.

There had certainly existed a small roundhouse at the eastern end of the fort, tucked in against a rock outcrop on which the fort wall had been built. The house was about 4.5m (15ft) across internally with stone-built walls and a central hearth. The hearth was paved and partially kerbed with stone slabs, and there were fragments of fired clay which may have been part of an oven.

Animal bones recovered by the excavations include those of cattle, sheep, pig and red deer, together with a single seal bone, providing a glimpse of the inhabitants' diet. Three glass beads were found, two yellow and one translucent with yellow spirals; such beads are common finds from settlements of the first century BC and the first two centuries AD throughout Britain, and they demonstrate that Iona's inhabitants were in trading contact with a wider world. Several hundreds of sherds of pottery were found, and, if a similar density of pottery may be assumed over the rest of the habitable areas of the fort, the total amount would be remarkably high. Analysis of the clay has revealed that the pottery was made locally in the island, but the shape and decoration of the vessels link it to a tradition widespread in

the Hebrides. These were rounded and bucket-shaped jars with out-turned rims, and some were decorated with zig-zag bands or fingertip impressions. The quantity of surviving pottery suggests that the fort was occupied over a long period, perhaps lasting into the third century AD. The fact that this distinctive pottery has been found only in Iona, Tiree, Coll and farther west and north may indicate that Iona's main links at this period were with the Hebrides rather than

15 Excavating the rampart of Dùn Bhuirg.

with mainland Argyll, but it is unfortunate that there has been no excavation on any of the Mull forts.

The location of the major monuments outside the Abbey complex is shown on the map (**16**). There are no traces of fortification on Dùn I, despite its suitability (**colour plates 3 and 4**). In his *Life of Columba*, Adomnán refers to the saint sitting 'on the little hill that is in Latin called "great fortress" [*munitio magna*]' (II, 4). In old Irish, the word *dùn* could mean either fortress or hill, and Adomnán's *munitio magna* could refer either to Dùn Bhuirg or to Dùn I. Given that Dùn I is both closer to the monastery and greater in height than Dùn Bhuirg, it seems likely that it was Dùn I on which Columba sat. Dùn I is an outsider's name for the hill, and it is likely that the original name was Dùn Mór, the Great Hill. It is not known whether Dùn Bhuirg was still in use in Columba's time.

Towards history

Ptolemy's survey of Scotland in the second century AD names the sea between Ireland, England and Scotland as Oceanus Ivernicus, from Ptolemy's name for Ireland, Ivernia. The Irish Sea it has remained to this day, and the implication is that its original Celtic name was also the Irish Sea, suggesting that it was in Iron Age times dominated by the Irish. There is certainly archaeological evidence for contacts between Ireland and Scotland from Neolithic times onwards, and from Roman times there is also historical evidence. Tacitus mentions that the Roman general Agricola gave shelter to an Irish prince in exile in north Britain in the first century AD, and it is also clear from his account that the Irish Sea was by then familiar to trading ships. Writing of Agricola's proposed invasion of Ireland, Tacitus relates that 'its approaches and harbours are known, through commerce and merchants' (*Agricola* 24). In the event, no Agricolan expedition to Ireland took place. Later Classical sources record that Scotti joined forces with the Picts against the Romans in the fourth century AD. (The Latin Scotti was simply a blanket

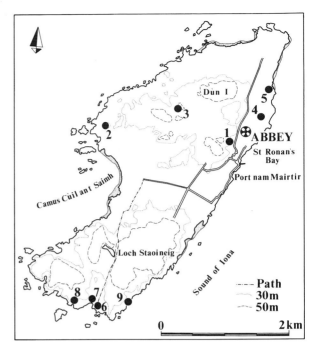

16 Map of sites in Iona outside the Abbey and Nunnery complex: 1 MacLean's Cross and Blàr Buidhe, 2 Dùn Bhuirg, 3 Cobhan Cùilteach, 4 Cladh an Dìsirt, 5 Port na Frainge, 6 Port na Curaich, 7 Port an Fhir-bhréige, 8 Làraichean, 9 marble quarry.

term for the inhabitants of Ireland (Scotia) rather than a reference to any particular tribe – the Irish called themselves Gaels.) The shortest crossing between the coast of County Antrim and the Mull of Kintyre was a mere 30km (18 miles), as a dramatic entry in the *Chronicon Scotorum* for around AD 700 illustrates: 'There was great frost in this year, so that the lakes and rivers of Ireland froze; and the sea froze between Ireland and Scotland, so that there was communication between them on sheet ice.'

Some of the Irish warriors who helped to harass the Roman army in north Britain may have stayed to settle in south-west Scotland. It is even possible that the Scotti allies of the Picts were already living in the west of Scotland, rather than having to cross the Irish Sea before marching eastwards to join the Pictish forces. There is certainly place-name evidence for an early and intensive settlement of Gaelic-speakers in the Rhinns of Galloway, in the form of names incorporating the element *sliabh*, meaning hill, and similar names are dotted along the north side of the Solway Firth, into the Firth of Clyde and in the islands of Islay and Jura. They cannot be dated precisely, but they may imply the presence of Gaelic-speaking settlers prior to the historical creation of the kingdom of Dalriada around AD 500. Archaeological evidence supports this sporadic Irish influence, not just with the occasional Irish type of artefact but also with the tradition of building souterrains, or earth-houses. These were stone-lined underground store-houses, and, although they were used in the early centuries AD in eastern Scotland, the few that have been found in Argyll are closer both geographically and architecturally to the many Irish examples. One has been found in Coll and another excavated at Kilellan in Islay. Some of the small stone forts of Argyll, especially those in Tiree, would look very familiar to settlers accustomed to cashels, the equivalent stone forts of Ireland.

The political situation in Scotland AD 400–600

Perhaps the most lasting effect of the presence of the Roman army in north Britain was to stimulate political unity among the Celtic tribes beyond the Forth and Clyde Rivers. Reflected in the commentaries of Classical authors of the second to fourth centuries is a picture of small tribes amalgamating into larger units more capable of organizing large-scale opposition to the Roman military threat. By the mid-sixth century, that process had evolved into the kingdom of the Picts, stretching from the Forth north to Shetland and west to the Outer Isles. South of the Forth and Clyde were British tribes, descended, like the Picts, from the earlier Celtic groups of the area, which in the West became the kingdom of Strathclyde and in the East became the Gododdin. In Argyll prior to about AD 500, the population is likely to have consisted of Britons in the South and Picts in the North, with an ever-increasing number of Irish newcomers. But it is really an anachronism to

think of the peasant majority of the population as either British or Pictish, as if they had a sense of nationality, for nationality is a relatively modern concept. It is more useful to think of their rulers as having a particular allegiance to British or Pictish overlords.

Around AD 500 there was a major political change in Argyll. For reasons that are barely understood but presumably related to political and territorial pressures in their homeland, the Irish tribe of Dál Riata transferred its ruling dynasty from its homeland in County Antrim to its growing colony in Argyll. This was no sudden mass migration, but rather a political decision and a small-scale movement of king and warlords. The king was Fergus Mór mac Erc, and for more than a century he and his successors ruled a kingdom split by the sea. That territorial kingdom is commonly known as Dalriada, and this is the term that will be used in this book, with Dál Riata retained in the strict sense of the people of the tribe of that name.

There are good documentary sources for the early history of Dalriada, in particular the *Annals of Ulster*, Adomnán's *Life of Columba* and the *Senchus Fer nAlban* (*History of the Men of Scotland*). Records kept in the monastery in Iona in the late seventh and early eighth centuries were incorporated into the *Annals of Ulster*, Adomnán was writing in the late seventh century, and the *Senchus* includes seventh-century material. According to the latter, there were three kindreds amongst the Dál Riata: the Cenél nGabran, who occupied Kintyre, Gigha and probably Jura, the Cenél nOengusa in Islay, and the Cenél Loairn, who held Lorn and lands north to Ardnamurchan and west to Coll and Tiree. Mull and Iona were thus within the territory of the kindred of Loairn. By the end of the seventh century another kindred had emerged in Cowal, the Cenél Comgaill. For almost two centuries, the overkings of Dalriada belonged to the Cenél nGabran, but the Cenél Loairn gained ascendancy from the late seventh to the mid-eighth century, finally relinquishing power again to the Cenél nGabran.

3
Columba and Iona

It was a familiar world into which Columba came to found his monastery. There were Gaelic-speakers in Argyll, and the landscape was already identified by many Gaelic place-names. Society was organized in the same way as in Ireland, contact with Ireland was frequent, and news travelled as fast as the currachs could sail across the North Channel. But was this a Christian world?

The beginnings of Christianity in Britain go back at least as early as the opening years of the third century, but its progress is not easy to chart, particularly in the fifth century. There were certainly Christian communities in Ireland by AD 431, when the Pope sent Palladius to act as their bishop, and a generation or so later St Patrick worked among the Irish; but overall the conversion appears to have been slow and sporadic. There is archaeological evidence for a Christian community at Whithorn in south-west Scotland around AD 400, and St Ninian was based there as bishop in the later fifth century. Paganism gave way to Christianity very gradually, more by example and word-of-mouth than by active missionary activity on the part of the Church. There can have been few Christians north of the Clyde–Forth line by AD 500, but some at least of the Dál Riata who settled in Argyll around that time are likely to have been converted before they left Ireland. The first historical King of Dalriada in Scotland, Domingart, 'withdrew into religion' towards the end of his life, according to the *Annals of Ulster*.

There is certainly no suggestion in any of the historical sources that the household of Conall, the King of the Dál Riata with whom Columba stayed on arrival, was anything other than Christian.

Columba's early life

Columba was born in County Donegal in AD 521 or 522 and died in Iona at the age of 75 on Sunday, 9 June 597. He belonged to the royal kin-group of the Cenél Conaill branch of the northern Uí Néill, and his family was to assume power over the Uí Néill in 566, after Columba had gone to Argyll. He was thus himself of noble blood, and his kinsmen were said to include kings of Tara, high kings of Ireland. His father was Fedilmid mac Ferguso and his mother was Eithne, and he had a brother and three sisters. It was the custom to send sons to be fostered by worthy individuals, and Columba was fostered by Cruithnechan, 'a priest of admirable life' (III, 2). Later tradition holds that Columba's original Irish name was Crimthann (fox), and it is possible that he took the name Columba (Latin, dove) on entering the Church. The Irish name Colum or Colm was relatively common, and thus in later times Columba became known as Colum Cille (church-dove) to distinguish him from the rest. His training for the Church began in boyhood with Cruithnechan, and in manhood, as a deacon, he studied under Bishop Finnio (or Finnen), perhaps at the monastery of Clonard in County Meath. Very little is known of his early career in Ireland until, in his early forties, Columba decided to leave Ireland and go to Scotland, 'wishing to be a pilgrim for Christ' in Adomnán's words (I, 4). Later medieval tradition attributed his departure from Ireland to a punishment for his supposed role in the battle of Cúl Drebene, in which the high king was defeated at the hands of Columba's kinsmen, but nothing is known with certainty about his connection with the battle. Máire Herbert has suggested that Columba may have left Ireland simply to avoid political entanglement and to get on with his life as a monk. Adomnán, ninth Abbot of Iona, wrote his *Life of Columba* sometime between AD 688 and 692, not quite a century after Columba's death, and it remains the most important source of information about the saint. It was not the first biography, for an earlier 'Book of the Miracles of Columba' was written by Cummene Find, seventh Abbot of Iona (657–69). This work was available to Adomnán, but it is now lost.

Columba came to Argyll in AD 563 with twelve companions, according to Adomnán. He appears first to have visited the High King of the Dál Riata, Conall mac Comgall, and to have stayed with him for some time. This was entirely appropriate to Columba's own noble lineage, but it was also an essential strategy to gain royal patronage. Negotiations may have been delicate in view of the fact that it was the territorial ambitions of Columba's kinsmen in the Northern Uí Néill that had led in part to the transfer of the ruling Dál Riata to Argyll. The question of how Columba acquired Iona is not easy to answer. Did he choose the island or was it chosen for him? Did he go straight to Iona after leaving Conall? The historical evidence is meagre and apparently conflicting. Adomnán makes no specific reference to the gift of Iona, but at the time of Conall's death in 574 the *Annals of Ulster* record that the king had given 'as an offering the island'. On the other hand, Bede relates that Iona 'long ago was resigned by gift of the Picts who inhabit those parts of Britain to monks of the Irish, through whose

teaching they had received the faith of Christ'. Bede goes on to record of Columba that 'by word and example he brought that nation [the Picts] to the faith of Christ. Therefore he received from them that island, to hold it for the making of a monastery ...' (III, 4). Was Iona gifted to Columba by Conall or by the Picts?

There is a good parallel in seventh-century Northumbria for the gift of royal land for the foundation of monasteries. The Northumbrian king Ecgfrith provided land from his own estates for the two monasteries of Jarrow and Monkwearmouth. Lindisfarne and Hexham were both supported by royal endowments. Yet it seems unlikely that Iona and Mull belonged to Conall, whose kindred territory was south of Lorn, unless his position as high king gave him rights over lands in other areas of Dalriada. Compared with the gifts to Jarrow and Monkwearmouth, the gift of land in Iona was tiny: Bede describes its area as 'about five hides', whereas Monkwearmouth was given seventy hides. A hide was the amount of land needed to support one family.

The Pictish king could certainly not have been involved in Dál Riata territory, but then Bede does not mention the king, only the Picts. One explanation may be that there was a Pictish bias to Bede's informant, or it may be that the native population of Mull and Iona still regarded itself as Pictish, for only fifty years or so had elapsed since the Dál Riata royal dynasty had transferred to Argyll. Perhaps Iona was the gift of a local chieftain, ratified by Conall.

A poem written by Dallán, a contemporary of Columba, sheds some light on the matter. In this poem, *Amra Choluimb Chille* (*The Elegy of Colum Cille*), Columba is described as 'not a hero unvigorous towards Conall's covenant', clearly a reference to an agreement between Columba and Conall, although Iona is not specifically mentioned. Columba also founded a monastery on an island known as Hinba, for which Jura is thought to be a likely candidate, and this could well have been a personal gift of royal land. Some of the earliest Gaelic place-

17 St Columba's Bay from the air; Port na Curaich with its long mound is in the centre of the photograph and Port an Fhir-bhréige with its pebble cairns is to the right.

names are to be found in Islay and Jura (those incorporating the element *sliabh*, hill). These two islands may have been the initial focus of settlement from Ireland.

There are several strongholds in Dalriada in which Conall could have been living at the time of Columba's visit. Monastic annals mention four by name: Dun Att (Dunadd near Lochgilphead), Dun Ollaigh (Dunollie on the north side of Oban Bay), Tairpert Boittir (Tarbert) and Aberte (Dunaverty at the south end of Kintyre). The last two were in the territory of the ruling Cenél

nGabran, but Conall could have been staying elsewhere for the purpose of collecting revenue in the form of livestock, grain and other commodities. Both Dunollie and Dunadd would have been suitable for the king and his retinue, particularly with their respective harbour facilities at Oban and Crinan for taking delivery of tribute from the islands.

Columba's arrival in Iona

Whether Columba set off to Iona from Jura or from mainland Argyll, his route is likely to have been along the south coast of Mull. St Columba's Bay at the south end of the island is traditionally the point at which the saint first landed in Iona (17). The bay has two beaches, separated by an outcrop of rock, Port an Fhir-bhréige with its pebble cairns to the west and Port na Curaich to the east. When Johnson and Boswell visited Iona in 1773, Port na Curaich was known to the islanders as Portawherry, 'from the wherry in which Columba came'. At that time, wherry was the standard term for a light rowing boat, but Boswell was interested to find that the islanders reverted to the Gaelic, currach, when showing him the length of Columba's vessel, 'as marked on the beach by two heaps of stones'. Earlier writers also describe two small piles of stones marking the length of the vessel, with no implication that the vessel itself was believed to be buried there. In one account written before 1701, the distance between the two heaps is described as 'three score of foots in length', 60ft or 18.3m, which is quite acceptable as the length of a seagoing currach in Columba's time. The single long mound on the beach today is thus likely to have been created, at least in part, in the early nineteenth century. Some 22m (72ft) long and

0.6m (2ft) high, the mound was excavated in 1878 and again in 1897, and proved to consist simply of pebbles.

Hide boats

The currach was a hide boat or skin boat, consisting of a light wooden frame covered with waterproof animal hide (**18**). Its use is likely to go back to early prehistoric times, but, being made of such highly perishable materials, it does not survive intact in the archaeological record. Fortunately there are many references to currachs in early documents, and visual evidence for them in the form of a model and a stone carving. The model was made in gold in the first century BC and found at Broighter on the banks of Lough Foyle in County Londonderry in Northern Ireland. It is tiny but detailed, and it has been estimated that it represents a seagoing hide boat of about 20m (66ft) in length. The carving is on a

18 Artist's impression of a sailing currach crewed by monks off the east coast of Iona.

tall stone pillar overlooking Bantry Bay in County Cork in south-west Ireland, and, like the gold model, shows both oars and steering oar, but here on a smaller currach crewed by eight oarsmen and a steersman.

Literary evidence for hide boats in use among the Celts in Britain goes back at least as early as the third century BC in the work of Classical authors. It is clear that these boats had a woven wicker framework and, most important in terms of their performance, they had a keel, which made them capable of long sea-journeys. Just how long may be judged from the voyage of St Brendan, who seems to have reached Iceland and possibly crossed the Atlantic. The account of his voyage includes a description of the boat:

St Brendan and his companions, using iron implements, prepared a currach, with wooden sides and ribs, such as is usually made in that country, and covered it with cow-hide tanned in oak-bark, tarring the joints thereof, and put on board provisions for forty days, with butter enough to dress hides for covering the boat, and all utensils needed for the use of the crew.

This paints a vivid picture of the wickerwork frame covered with cow-hides, the seams sealed with pitch, and of the need to take extra butter on the voyage to keep the hides waterproof. The sail is not mentioned, but it would have been part of the design.

If Columba's currach was indeed 20m (66ft) long, its construction would have needed some twenty hides, and it could have had a crew of eighteen oarsmen and a steersman, along with a considerable amount of luggage. In an addition to the original manuscript of his *Life of Columba*, Adomnán records that twelve men sailed with Columba. Of the twelve names only three are mentioned in the main text of the *Life*, and the number may be an allusion to the twelve Apostles. Even if there were twelve companions, there may well have been other attendants whose names were not recorded. The *Senchus Fer*

nAlban refers to seven-benched boats, which would have needed fourteen oarsmen, and this may have been the most common size of boat.

There were other types of boat in use in Scotland at this period, but the hide boat appears to have been the normal choice for Irishmen. Amongst the Picts, wooden plank-built vessels and logboats were more common, to judge by carved representations and the only boat of Early Historic date to have survived, a logboat dated by radiocarbon analysis (in the McManus Galleries, Dundee). But plank-built boats were certainly in use in Dalriada by the seventh century. Adomnán records an occasion in his own time when a wooden longship was built in Iona, using imported and ready-dressed timbers of oak and pine (II, 45), and this was clearly not an isolated event. He also refers to a smaller type of hide boat, *scafa*, which may have been more like the modern coracle used on rivers than the seagoing currach.

The Columban monastery

Only rarely in Scottish archaeology before the twelfth century is there the luxury of having any written description of what the spade may uncover. Iona is a special case. Although Adomnán was not concerned with describing the monastery either in Columba's day or in his own, he mentions many details which allow a picture of the monastic buildings to be pieced together. There is little sense of their layout, however, and the reconstruction drawing of the monastery at the end of the eighth century (see 67) is entirely conjectural. Adomnán refers to a church with a side-chamber or chapel, and to sleeping-places (*cubicula*) for the monks. These sleeping-places may have been either individual huts or compartments within a larger building or dormitory. Two buildings were used by Columba himself; the first was his sleeping-place, where he had 'for his couch, the bare rock, and for his pillow a stone', and the second was his writing-place. There was also a communal building for the monks, probably where meals were prepared and consumed, and a guest-house.

19 The grave-marker known as 'St Columba's Pillow' dates from some two centuries after Columba's time.

Beyond the main complex were barns and a building interpreted as a corn-drying kiln. Although the individual buildings are not described in detail, there are references scattered throughout the *Life* to gathering reeds for thatching and to importing timber and wattles for building, and it is clear that wooden planks and wattle (presumably covered with clay) were the primary building materials (see pp. 40, 53).

Adomnán mentions several burials, including that of Columba himself, and this implies the presence of a graveyard within the monastery grounds. Columba's grave was marked by the stone that he had used as a pillow (III, 23). In the Abbey museum, still inside the iron cage made to protect it in the nineteenth century, there is a gravestone popularly known as St Columba's Pillow (no. 60). In fact, of all the pillow-stones in the Iona collection, this is probably the least likely candidate to have been the original Columban stone, because the type of ringed cross carved upon it dates no earlier than the eighth century (**19**). Sadly there is no way of identifying the saint's gravestone. Later tradition links the

famous Stone of Destiny with Iona as Columba's pillow-stone, but this is likely to be wishful thinking. The Stone, described by Neal Ascherson as 'a great blind slab of Dark Ages magic', was removed from Scotland by King Edward I, and from the early fourteenth century it lay below the seat of the coronation chair in Westminster Abbey in London. The formal decision to return it to Scotland was taken in 1996. The Stone of Destiny has no historical context earlier than its use at Scone for royal inauguration ceremonies, and the traditional link with Iona cannot be proved. Moreover, the Stone is made of a type of sandstone found in the Perthshire area.

Adomnán makes just one reference to the monastic vallum, the earthwork enclosing the monastery, but does not provide any detail about its appearance or extent (II, 29).

The early monastic enclosure

The vallum is the most impressive structural element of the early monastery which is still visible today, particularly the stretch at the north-west corner of the enclosure, beyond Burnside Cottage (**20**; **colour plates 5 and 6**; see A on the plan, **21**). Here the earthwork consists of an inner bank about 1.8m (6ft) high, a ditch and an outer bank some 1.2m (4ft) high, and the drop from the top of the inner bank to the present bottom of the ditch is fully 4m (13ft). The banks are eroded and the ditch partly filled with silt, and the earthwork in its original state was clearly very substantial. Another well-preserved section lies on the west side of Cnoc nan Càrnan (**22**), and a trench dug across it in 1956 showed that the ditch had been dug into solid rock, underlining the scale of the task involved in creating the vallum (see D on **21**). It was over 4m (13ft) wide, but unfortunately its original depth could not be discovered, because the lower part was water-logged. Both ramparts were about 4m (13ft) wide and built of stones and earth, and an old turf-line within the inner rampart suggested that it had been renewed or heightened on at least one occasion in the past. The whole earthwork was thus some 12m (39ft) wide and, if the inner

20 The Abbey from the air showing the line of the monastic vallum.

rampart was topped with a wooden fence, its height may have been quite considerable.

The extent of the monastic enclosure is best appreciated from the air (see **20**) and on plan (see **21**), as a large sub-rectangular area with an annexe at the south end. Intensive cultivation south of the Abbey has masked all trace of the enclosure even from the air, but geophysical survey has revealed a complex of buried ditches (see G, H, J on **21**). A trench excavated at J in the grounds of the St Columba Hotel in 1973 confirmed the presence of a ditch 3m (10ft) wide and more than 2m (6ft) deep. These ditches reflect a complicated history in the evolution of the vallum and its annexe over a number of centuries, and only an intensive campaign of research excavations will sort out the sequence.

The picture is further confused by the need for substantial drainage ditches, remains of which may be mistaken for enclosure ditches. A layer of impermeable clay lies beneath the glacial sand and causes problems with surface water; drainage ditches dug from Iron Age times onwards have been found in excavations. Yet another factor is an overburden of imported 'garden soil', up to 2m (6ft) thick, which appears to have been brought into the later medieval monastic enclosure in an effort to improve the quality of the soil for cultivation.

The main enclosure gives the appearance of having been open to the sea along its east side, but in fact its perimeter lay along the scarp of the raised beach, which was probably heightened artificially. Timber stockades and even thorn hedges are known to have been used in Ireland. There would be little point in building a strong vallum on three sides and leaving the fourth

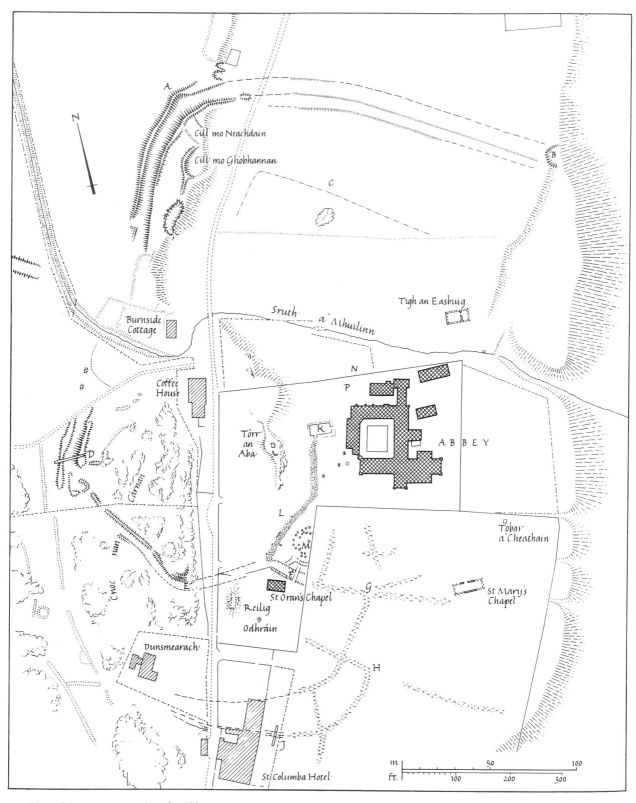

21 Plan of the area surrounding the Abbey.

unprotected. At its maximum extent, the area of the main monastic enclosure was thus about 8ha (20 acres), with perhaps another hectare bounded by the annexe. In Ireland, most early monastic enclosures were round or oval, but a few, like Iona, were rectangular.

But as yet only one small section of one of these lines of earthworks at Iona can be dated. In 1979 a team led by John Barber excavated for Historic Scotland part of the ditch identified by Ian Fisher as the southern boundary of the

22 The vallum on Cnoc nan Càrnan.

23 Excavations north of Reilig Odhráin in 1979; the Columban ditch lies in the middle foreground (with a T-shaped arrangement of measuring rods in front of it), and the edge of the seventh-century vallum is visible at an early stage in its excavation in the foreground.

main enclosure (see M on **21**; **23**). The reason for the dig was that the burial-ground of Reilig Odhráin was to be extended to the north of St Oran's Chapel – the triangular extension that can be seen today. Again the problem of water-logging was encountered, but here it turned into a major advantage, because the wet conditions had preserved organic materials such as leather and wood, which normally rot away. The ditch proved to be 5–6m (16–19ft) wide and almost 3m (10ft) deep, and samples of peat and wood from the ditch bottom suggest that it was in existence in the period AD 600–35. It replaced an earlier and smaller ditch dated to the Columban period proper. This was about 2m (6ft 6in) wide and 1.2m (4ft) deep, but its meandering course is difficult to reconcile with interpretation as the first monastic vallum. Nevertheless its scale is, as John Barber points out in his report, consistent with the labouring capabilities of a small pioneering community.

There seems to have been an entrance through the larger ditch of seventh-century date beneath the line of the later medieval Street of the Dead, and it may be that the line of this vallum continued north-westwards and utilized the east face of Cnoc nan Càrnan as part of its western course. If the lines of ditch between E and H on the plan were linked originally across Reilig Odhráin, the cross-base in the latter might, as Ian Fisher suggested, mark an entrance through an outer vallum. If so, it would line up with the entrance through the excavated ditch.

Immediately to the north of the two ditches excavated beneath the modern extension to the cemetery, the same 1979 excavation revealed the post-holes of perhaps half of a circular wooden structure. Its architecture and function were far from clear, and its date could be anywhere between the early seventh and the eleventh centuries. If it was a building, the diameter of its main wall was about 14m (46ft), and there was some sort of verandah or outer storage area around it. There was a change from predominantly circular to predominantly rectangular buildings in secular contexts in

Ireland in the course of the eighth and ninth centuries, although in Pictland the equivalent change began rather earlier. If this circular structure at Iona was some sort of domestic building, its circular plan would not be surprising in an essentially Irish context.

Traces of the early monastic buildings

Most of the twentieth-century excavations have been, and continue to be, carried out in response to restoration projects around the Abbey and Nunnery, whether within buildings or in external areas where service facilities are to be laid. There was a phase of excavation purely for research needs, which was financed by the Russell Trust and took place mainly in the late 1950s and 1960s. But from 1979 onwards, in keeping with archaeological policy elsewhere in Scotland, the emphasis has been on rescue operations ahead of necessary building work. Now, at the turn of the second millennium AD, we know enough about the monastery of Iona to ask the right questions and to devise a campaign of excavations to answer them. All that is needed is funding!

Not every trench sunk into Iona soil produces archaeology, even around the Abbey, and this is not the place for a blow-by-blow account of every small area opened by the spade. But some have produced information about the early monastery. Beneath the medieval bakehouse (see K on the plan, **21**) was found a mass of about 60 post-holes, which were very difficult to fit into any coherent pattern but could possibly be the remains of a rectangular building. Radiocarbon dates from the layer of soil sealing the older post-holes suggest that the timber building that they represent is likely to be eighth century or earlier in date. Post-holes and slots were also found in front of the west front of the Abbey church, but no pattern could be made of them.

South of Tòrr an Aba (at L on the plan), excavations uncovered traces of a bedding-trench for a plank-built structure, but there was no clue as to its date. It cut through a red layer which was at first interpreted as the result of intense burning and related to the Viking raids of the late eighth to tenth centuries, but this red material was later proved to be the remains of rotted seaweed lying on the ancient raised beach.

Tòrr an Aba

Adomnán describes Columba's writing-hut as 'constructed on higher ground' (III, 22), and it has reasonably been suggested that the hut was on the rocky outcrop traditionally known as Tòrr an Aba (Hill of the Abbot), west of the Abbey (**colour plate 7**). There has been much scholarly argument about this hut, because Adomnán also refers to the saint sitting 'in tegoriolo tabulis subfulto' (I, 25). The phrase has been variously interpreted as 'in the hut that was supported on planks' or 'in his raised wooden hut', which suggest that the building was either supported on a raft of joists or raised up on piles above boggy ground. Combined with the reference to higher ground, the former seems more likely, and the uneven top of the Tòrr might call for a level wooden foundation. There are a couple more clues from Adomnán's account. Columba could see Mull from inside his hut and could hear shouting from the other side of the Sound of Iona, both of which are possible from Tòrr an Aba.

Excavations in 1956 and 1957 add a physical dimension to the discussion. Remains were found of a massively built stone revetment along the foot of the west side of the Tòrr; if this had extended upwards, its purpose was probably to increase the usable space on the top of the outcrop. On the top, beside a later medieval cross-base, excavation revealed the remains of rough stone foundations of a sub-rectangular building, with an internal floor space of about 2.8 by 3.8m (9 by 12ft). Fragments of burnt stakes, about a centimetre in diameter, along the footing of the west wall led the excavators, Elizabeth and Peter Fowler, to suggest that the stone base had been topped with turf, which supported either a low wattle wall or a 'wigwam' roof. Inside, the floor area was very

irregular, dropping in parts to 0.6m (2ft) or more. At one end, the surface of the bedrock had been shaped to form a low 'bench', and there was a setting of stone slabs forming a box about 0.8m (2ft 7in) long, which was interpreted as the support for a stone or wooden 'table-top'. The building was later demolished, and its interior levelled with a fill of earth and beach-pebbles. The stone plinth for the medieval cross-base was built partly overlapping this pebble fill. Both the cross-base and the line of the hut-foundations are visible today.

Unfortunately there is no dating evidence for any part of this sequence. The location seems reasonable for Adomnán's 'higher ground', but do the excavated remains fit Adomnán's description? Were it not for the stone box, one would be tempted to argue that the very irregular interior of the building was not the original floor, but that wooden joists spanned it and supported a floor at a higher level. But the box, and indeed the stone 'bench', sound most unlikely constructions at a period when, as we shall see, Iona's monastic carpenters were dressing timbers for sophisticated wooden buildings and carving lathe-turned bowls. The answer may be that the box and 'bench' belong to some earlier, pre-monastic, phase of activity. If they are dropped from the equation, the stone wall-footings can be interpreted as supporting the wooden joists for Columba's wooden writing-hut.

When the timbers rotted beyond repair, the hut was demolished and the site levelled with earth and pebbles. Why? Not for the medieval cross-plinth, which barely overlaps it, but perhaps for some building which no longer survives (see **40**).

Workshops

In keeping with the self-sufficient life-style of a monastery, traces have been found of open-air workshops for metalworking and glassworking. On the north side of the Abbey (see P on **21**) were found patches of cobbling and evidence of burning, which are likely to represent industrial

24 Clay moulds for making glass studs with interlaced metal inlays.

activities. These were certainly part of the early monastery, because they produced a sherd of imported pottery (E-ware) and three clay moulds for making inlaid glass studs, probably in the eighth century (24). There was also a tiny bronze bell with a clapper inside, which is an appropriate piece of equipment for a monastery. Adomnán refers to a bell that was struck to summon the monks together (I, 8), but this would have been a much larger bell, probably struck with a baton rather than rung with a clapper. More evidence of early metalworking came from excavations inside the Abbey museum; there were no structural traces, but two fragments of small triangular crucibles were found, along with the lug or handle from a crucible. Crucibles of this sort were used to melt the small amounts of bronze needed for brooches and pins. They were lying in the layer of 'garden soil' brought into the Abbey grounds

in medieval times, and could have come from anywhere in the vicinity. There was also a sherd of Roman pottery, which probably belonged to the Iron Age inhabitants of the island. From the area excavated north of Reilig Odhráin came a piece of glass rod ready for use as inlay, blue-green in colour with a fine trail of yellow glass spiralling round it.

The imported pottery may seem out of place in Iona's self-sufficient monastery, but it may well have arrived there as gifts. The type known to archaeologists as E-ware was made in south-west France in the late sixth and early seventh centuries, and another sherd found just outside the north boundary wall of the Abbey belongs to the rim of a large bowl made in north Africa in the late fifth and early sixth centuries. The latter is a rare find in the British Isles, and Iona is by far its most northerly known destination, whereas E-ware is more common and has been found on a number of Scottish sites as far north as the Moray Firth. In both cases, the pottery vessels are likely to have held exotic commodities and to have been a side-line for merchants primarily involved in the wine trade. Adomnán mentions a ship arriving in Argyll from Gaul in Columba's time (I, 28), thus providing invaluable historical support for the archaeologists' sherds of imported pottery (see p. 48). There was clearly a far-ranging trade network available in the sixth to eighth centuries, with ships sailing north through the Irish Sea to bring wine, olive oil and other goods in exchange for fine hides, wool and, from lay communities, slaves.

The two ditches found in the area excavated on the north side of Reilig Odhráin had been used as convenient dumps from nearby carpentry and leather workshops, and the damp conditions in the ditches preserved both wood and leather. There was debris from turning bowls on a simple lathe, together with parts of three fine bowls, mostly made of alder (**25**). There were also remains of structural timbers, including evidence for using posts and panels set into horizontal sill-beams, together with part of a stave-built barrel. Wood was also used for pegs, spatulas, spoons, handles and a walking stick. Apart from part of a purse, the leather was all from shoemaking, and it forms a very important group of material illustrating shoe fashion at a period for which there is otherwise little evidence. These were shoes made out of several pieces, with a tongue at the front and occasionally at the heel. This style of shoe can be seen depicted in a number of illustrated manuscripts of the period, most notably on the stylized figure symbolizing St Matthew in the *Book of Durrow*, created in the late seventh century.

All the excavated evidence for early buildings comes from within the area of the main monastic enclosure, but it is as yet impossible to be certain where the focus of the Columban monastery lay. On balance, it seems likely that the early church stood roughly on the same spot as the later Abbey church, otherwise it is difficult to explain why the great high crosses of the eighth century should be positioned outside

the west end of the later church. Traces of earlier foundations were found beneath the nave during restoration work, but they could not be identified with confidence.

The evidence from Iona fits well with what is known of contemporary monasteries in Ireland. In the west of Ireland, where stone was the natural building material, the form of the monastic enclosure shows that sometimes, as at Iona, there were annexes and subdivisions within the enclosures. These divisions could reflect differing degrees of sanctity within the main enclosure, or simply separate areas set aside for specialized activities, such as the graveyard, industrial workshops or guest-house. The main focus of any monastery was the church, and here the Irish evidence shows that over the centuries the number of churches in a single monastery could grow. Rather than rebuild or enlarge an existing church, it was quite common practice to build another, whether in wood or later in stone. This is perhaps a feature that we should be prepared to find at Iona. The most remarkable feature of many Irish monasteries from the tenth to thirteenth centuries was the round stone tower, but this idea was rarely imported into Scotland (the only such towers surviving are those in eastern Scotland at Abernethy and Brechin).

25 Lathe-turned wooden bowl decorated with horizontal lines.

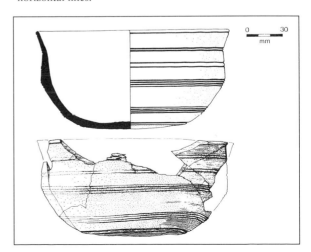

There may, however, have been earlier watchtowers built of timber (see p. 92). Unfortunately little detail is known about the Columban monasteries in Ireland, although excavation is gradually filling out the picture of monasteries in general. The great monastery of Kells was founded from Iona at the start of the ninth century, and it came to be furnished with a round tower as well as three high crosses and a small stone church known as 'Columcille's House', all of which survive today.

The monastic economy

Adomnán mentions cows and the milking of cows in Columba's time. Barley was grown, and threshing the grain and baking bread are mentioned in passing. Other animals and foods, such as deer, apples and nuts, come into some of the stories of the saint's miracles, but they all take place outside Iona, as does river fishing. Archaeological evidence from excavations supports the breeding of cattle, sheep, goats and pigs and the cultivation of cereals, and it also points to the products of deer-hunting, fowling and fishing coming to the monastery. Hake and cod were caught, and limpets, winkles, whelks and oysters were collected. Seals may have been hunted, for Adomnán mentions 'the little island that is the breeding-place of the seals we reckon as our own' (I, 41).

Beeswax was needed for the wax tablets on which much everyday writing was done, but there is no clue as to whether bees were kept in Iona or whether the wax was imported. Illustrated gospel-books and other manuscripts were written on vellum, for which calf-skin was required, preferably from calves not older than three months. An average manuscript could involve 25–80 animals (one skin for every two folios or pages), and a monastery such as Iona with active scribes had to maintain a substantial herd of cattle in order to keep up the supply of skins. Hides from adult animals were also required for clothing, bedding, shoes and hide boats, although animals other than cattle could be used as well. The leather found in

excavations at Iona ranged from calf and cow to goat, horse, red deer and seal.

Iona's herb garden

In a fascinating book about traditional medicines in the Highlands and Islands of Scotland, Mary Beith suggests that the medicine practised by monks in the Early Christian period included pre-Christian cures and even incantations (1995). Aside from spiritual healing, Adomnán credits Columba with expertise in dealing with nosebleeds, fractures and blindness. Medicine called for the judicious use of herbs, and every monastery would have had its herb garden in which both herbs and vegetables were grown. Mary Beith suggests that some idea of Iona's herb garden may be gleaned from the records made around 820 of the herb garden of the monastery of St Gall in Switzerland, founded a century before by Irish monks. Over thirty plants were listed, including pepperwort, costmary, fenugreek, rosemary, mint, sage, rue, pennyroyal, watercress, cumin, lovage, fennel, onion-leaf celery, coriander, dill, poppies, parsley, chervil, climbing beans, radishes, beet, garlic, shallots, lettuce, parsnip and cabbage. Early Irish tracts on healing emphasize the properties of garlic and celery in particular, and plant remains from modern excavations have added lovage to the list. These could all have been grown in Iona with some protection. The land enclosed within the vallum was far larger than needed simply for the buildings of the monastery, and a herb garden or vegetable plot, an apple orchard and a soft-fruit garden are likely to have been included in its grounds.

Iomaire Tochair

To the north-west of the monastery was a loch, some 8ha (20 acres) in extent, known as Lochan Mór or the Big Lochan (a lochan is a small loch or lake). This was drained around 1750 in order to provide a source of peat for the islanders. Prominent even today is a flat-topped grassy embankment, which runs dead straight along the

26 The circular stone foundation of Cobhan Cùilteach and, in the background on the left, the walled enclosure.

south-west side of Lochan Mór. This is known as Iomaire Tochair, which means Ridge of the Causeway. It appears to be of great antiquity and has fuelled much speculation as to its purpose, but its name should probably be taken literally and its function seen as that of a raised causeway which allowed access along the boggy margin of Lochan Mór into the higher ground. This would give convenient access across the island to the north end of the machair, and the causeway could have been built at any time after the monastery was fully established. The monastic vallum shows the earth-moving labours of which the community was capable.

Cobhan Cùilteach

'One day, when St Columba was living on Iona, he set off into the wilder parts of the island to find a place secluded from other people where he could pray alone' (III, 8). No building is mentioned, nor is any necessary for prayer, yet this passage has become associated with the remains of an oval stone hut in the interior of the island, west of Dùn I and about 1km (0.6 mile) from the monastery (26). This is a prime example of 'the past as wished for' and the natural desire to locate tangible places and artefacts with Columba. In sober fact, the building has not been excavated and there is no means of dating it. Its name has often been translated as the Hermit's Cell or even the Culdee's Cell, although the Gaelic really means no more than the Remote Hollow, and the name was probably invented to imply a connection with Columba's secluded place for prayer.

Nevertheless, it is an interesting building, whatever its date. It consists of rough stone foundations for an oval hut, about 4.6 by 3.4m (15 by 11ft) within a wall almost a metre thick.

There is an entrance on the south-west side. This is the most common orientation for the entrances into prehistoric hut-circles in Scotland, because it allowed the maximum light into the house from the open door (an important consideration in buildings without windows). The stone foundations could have supported walls of turf or timber, or, if stone has been removed to build field walls, it could have had a corbelled dome of 'beehive' type. It is sheltered to the north by the rocky outcrop of Cnoc nam Bradhan, and attached to the west end of the outcrop is an enclosure, about 25 by 12m (82 by 39ft) internally, built of boulders of cyclopean dimensions. Some of these huge stones may have been deliberately quarried from the adjacent rock-face. Again there is no way of estimating its age, or of knowing whether it is contemporary with the oval hut. There are remains of a small rectangular building in the north-west corner, which looks more recent than the main wall and suggests that the enclosure has been used in relatively recent times as a pen for sheep or cattle. But its origins could be much earlier.

A church for the lay population?

One of the most intriguing results of excavations in recent years in Iona is the proof of a lay population in early Christian times and the possibility of a church serving that lay population. Jerry O'Sullivan excavated within the shell of St Ronan's Church in 1992, on behalf of the Iona Cathedral Trust and in advance of the renovation work that has transformed the ruin into a museum of medieval stone sculpture. The surviving building dates to the twelfth or thirteenth century and was the parish church for Iona. Beneath its floor lay traces of an earlier and smaller church, which may have been its predecessor as the church used by the lay population, who would probably only on special occasions worship in the church inside the monastery. This earlier church was built with clay-bonded walls, plastered with lime mortar, and these techniques, combined with the dedication to St Ronan, suggest a date no earlier than the eighth century. St Ronan is thought to have been an eighth-century Abbot of St Blane's monastery on the island of Bute. The position of the earlier walls is marked by pink granite slabs incorporated into the modern paving of St Ronan's Church.

Even before this small church was built, there was an early Christian cemetery on the site. The graves of nine people were revealed within the excavated area, and there are likely to be more outside. They were buried in simple pits long enough to take each body, orientated east–west in the Christian manner, but unfortunately soil conditions were against the preservation of bone and the skeletal remains were too fragmentary to allow identification of age or sex. But, if the church is as early as the eighth century, these graves prove that there was a lay population in Iona in early Christian times.

4
Iona and Dalriada

The choice of the island of Iona, on the fringe of Dalriada, for Columba's monastery may reflect a deliberate distancing between Columba and the royal house of the Dál Riata. After all, Columba belonged to the Northern Uí Neill tribe, whose dynastic and territorial ambitions had led to the transfer of the royal dynasty of the Dál Riata to Argyll. His monastery maintained close links with the homeland in Ireland, and no fewer than six of the eight abbots who succeeded Columba at Iona over the next 107 years were also of the same Cenél Conaill branch of the Northern Uí Néill. Relations between Iona and the kings of Dál Riata were bound to be somewhat cautious. The importance of Columba's monastery was apparently soon recognized, for Aedán mac Gabráin, Conall's successor, was ordained King of the Dál Riata by Columba at Iona in AD 574 (*Life of Columba*, III, 5). Aedán outlived Columba, and therefore Adomnán was not concerned to record in the *Life* whether Aedán's successor, Eochaid Buide, or indeed subsequent kings, were also ordained at Iona. This point is of some importance because, as we shall see, there is reason to believe that regional kings, if not high kings, held initiation ceremonies at the secular stronghold of Dunadd. It may be that, as the Dál Riata were gradually converted, only high kings were given the additional authority of being ordained in an ecclesiastical setting.

Within Dalriada, Iona's status appears to have been high from the beginning, and it was not long before the influence of Iona reached out into Pictland and Northumbria. Scholarly opinion is divided as to the degree to which Iona, and Columba in particular, had a missionary role. Adomnán stresses the importance of Columba within his own community and within the Iona family of monastic houses, but he was writing primarily for that same audience and may not have been interested in presenting the external missionary aspect. He mentions four dependent houses or hermitages established from Iona: Mag Luinge in Tiree, Hinba, Cella Diuni near Loch Awe, and an island named Elen. Hinba is thought to be Jura, and the likeliest place in the island is the church-site at Cill Earnadil in the most fertile part of the island. The name Earnadil may reflect the name of Columba's uncle, Ernan, who is known to have been Prior of Hinba for a short time. Cella Diuni may have been close to the point at which the River Awe flows out of the loch, for there the place-name Annat indicates an early ecclesiastical site. The island of Elen remains unknown, but it is likely to have been within Dalriada. A strong candidate is Eileach an Naoimh in the Garvellachs, but Nave Island off the north coast of Islay is another possibility, where there are remains of an early church-site. All these sites and the Tiree evidence will be discussed in Chapter 7.

Even more difficult to establish is the provision made for worship and burial among the lay population of the Dál Riata. This will have depended upon the patronage of wealthy families, and in the early days of Christianity both churches and prayer-crosses are likely to have been made of perishable wood rather than stone. It is not until the eighth century that the great stone crosses were created, presumably with lay patronage, at places like Kilnave or, most splendid of all, Kildalton (see **53**, **54**; see also pp. 76–8). The fort at Dunadd and its rural population may have been served by churches at Kilmichael Glassary and Kilmartin, where early Christian graveslabs survive, and, at Kilmartin, a free-standing cross of ninth- or tenth-century date. A famous bell-shrine was found at Kilmichael Glassary; the shrine itself was created in the twelfth century, but the iron bell within it is older. The monastery founded on Lismore in the sixth century by St Moluag is likely to have benefited by the seventh and eighth centuries from the lay patronage of wealthy inhabitants of the fort at Dunollie.

Royal strongholds in Dalriada

Columba had a vision of a disaster that had befallen a city in Italy, and his vision was confirmed two or three months later when news of the disaster was brought by sailors from Gaul (France). According to Adomnán, Columba and his companion, Luigbe, had gone to 'the capital of the district', where Luigbe 'questioned the master and sailors of a ship that arrived' (I, 28). On current evidence, the most likely candidate

for that 'capital' in the sixth and seventh centuries is the fort of Dunadd, where excavation has yielded evidence of high-status trade and exchange. Dunadd is a large rocky hill, which rises abruptly above flat boggy land (boggier then than now) north of modern Lochgilphead (**27**). Although it is close to the River Add, which runs into the sea at Loch Crinan, Dunadd is most unlikely to have been the port at which the ship arrived. The river executes some spectacular meanders over the 8.5km (5.3 miles) or so between the sea and the fort, and treacherously narrow channels through the mudflats at the head of Loch Crinan would have had to be navigated before the river was reached. It is more likely that the port was in the same location as Crinan Harbour today, on the south side of the mouth of Loch Crinan. Goods could then have been transported either by small boats along the Add or, more probably, overland, by skirting the water-logged Moine Mhór and approaching Dunadd from the south-east.

But in many ways the stronghold of Dunollie at Oban is far better placed as a trading station, for ships could put in to Port Mór to the immediate south. Excavations have yielded only a fraction of the prestigious objects found at Dunadd, but equally the area examined at Dunollie is a fraction of that investigated at Dunadd. It must also be admitted that neither

27 The fort at Dunadd occupies the summit and terraces of a rocky hill.

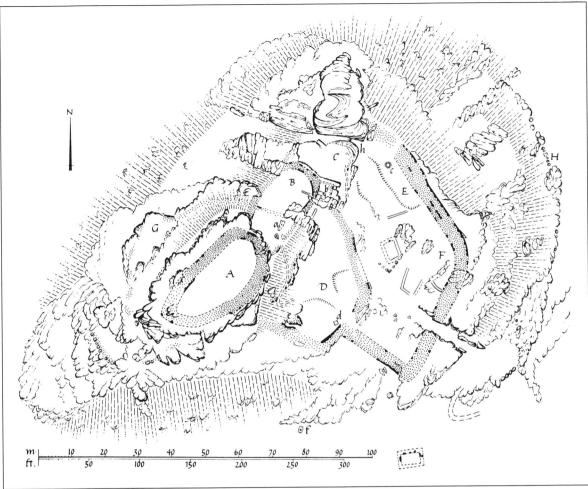

28 The plan of the fort at Dunadd: A citadel, B–F lower enclosures, (a) carved rock face.

site has produced finds dating as early as the time of Columba, though both were occupied in Adomnán's lifetime and may well have been flourishing earlier. In both cases, the earliest fortification is likely to have been relatively small, and there are other small forts dated by archaeological means to the seventh century which may also be candidates for 'the capital of the district'.

The fort at Dunadd

The potential importance of Dunadd has been recognized since at least the mid-nineteenth century. Scholars identified the Dùn At mentioned twice in the *Annals of Ulster* as the hill of Dunadd in Mid Argyll, and the site became an obvious target for excavation. In fact, some fifty years were to pass before the first campaign of excavation in 1904–5; another took place in 1929. Both produced large numbers of artefacts but little information about where precisely they had been found, and this prompted further excavations by Alan Lane in 1980–1.

The hill rises to a height of 54m (177ft) above sea-level and consists of bare outcrops of rock with reasonably level terraces between them. The fort-builders made the most of the natural shape of the hill by creating a small enclosure or citadel at the highest point and a series of walled terraces below, but this final plan seems to have been achieved in stages over perhaps two centuries (**28**). The summit fort was originally oval, about 20 by 13m (66 by

43ft) in area, surrounded by a stone wall, and it had first been built sometime in the last few centuries BC. It was later extended on the south-west into a pear-shape, and by the seventh century, this had become the citadel of a more extensive fort. Allowing for the rocky outcrops, it has been estimated that the fort in its final form enclosed some 2500 square metres (2990 square yards) of usable space, subdivided into areas designated for various purposes. One of these was certainly a workshop for metalworking, and others would have included domestic houses, stables and barns, while the citadel would have contained the great feasting-hall. The entrance to the fort lay in a natural cleft in the bedrock, which would have been strengthened by massive walling on either side

and probably a timber superstructure over a double gate (**29**).

Outside the entrance to the summit fort, there is a remarkable set of carvings. A circular basin, 0.25m (10in) across and 0.14m (5in) deep, has been hollowed into the solid rock, along with two 'footprints', set 2m (6ft 7in) apart but on roughly the same alignment (**30**). These are the shallow outlines of shod feet, and they and the basin are thought to relate to royal initiation ceremonies. It is unfortunate that they cannot be dated. They could have originated in Iron Age times, but the fact that the same rock surface bears other carvings of certain Dark Age date implies that their significance was at least still understood at that period. There is a strong possibility that they were still used in ceremonies surrounding the initiation of kings.

The later carvings consist of a fine Pictish-style boar and an inscription in ogham letters.

29 Looking through the entrance into enclosure D to the outer enclosure and the main entrance into the fort.

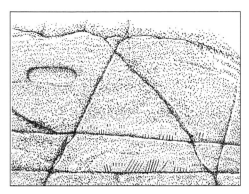

30 One of the footprints and the ogham inscription at Dunadd.

The boar may symbolize a marriage alliance between a Dál Riata leader and a Pictish princess. The *Annals of Ulster* record that in 736 the Pictish king Aengus son of Fergus captured Dunadd, but, if the boar was carved in commemoration of that victory, the Dál Riata would surely have obliterated it once they regained possession of the fort. Ogham was invented in Ireland as a convenient alphabet for carving on wood and stone, and it was probably introduced into Dalriada and Pictland by Irish missionaries. The Dunadd inscription has yet to be translated, but it is likely to be in Irish and to record personal names. The fort is in state care, and the whole of the carved surface, except for the basin, is covered by a protective layer and topped with a cast of the original carvings. Close to the tail of the boar, there is also a twentieth-century carving of a man in profile smoking a pipe, with an inscription that reads 'King Fergus' – cut by someone with a misplaced sense of humour.

Dunadd is not alone in its footprint carvings. Another may be seen at Southend in the Mull of Kintyre, near the fort at Dunaverty which is thought to be the Aberte mentioned in the annals (the second footprint at Southend is modern). There are pairs of footprints at the Iron Age fortified settlement of Clickhimin in Shetland and in Orkney on a large boulder now kept in the church at Burwick in South Ronaldsay. Late medieval records describe kingly initiation ceremonies involving

footmarked stones both in western Scotland and Ireland, and it appears that the tradition was in origin much older. The Lords of the Isles were proclaimed at a ceremony which included placing a foot in a carved footprint, in order to show that the new Lord would walk in the footsteps of his predecessors.

There is no problem in envisaging essentially pagan initiation ceremonies alongside Christian ordination, for the early Church was open to reasonable compromise. There are no historical records concerning the ordaining of Dál Riatan kings other than Aedán, but it may well be that kings were created both in the eyes of the Church and also according to lay tradition.

But what of daily life at Dunadd? The various campaigns of excavation have produced a wide range of information, with the exception of organic remains, for which the soil conditions were unfavourable. There are no artefacts of wood or leather or even of bone, and few animal bones to illuminate the meat element in the diet of the inhabitants. To judge by sites of comparable date, cattle would have been the most important item, followed by pigs, sheep, goats and deer. There are plant remains preserved by burning, enough to show that wheat, barley, oats and hazelnuts figured in the diet. An extraordinary aspect of the equipment that survived was the number of quernstones, of which more than fifty were found. These were parts of rotary hand-querns, each of which has an upper and a lower stone. They represent the endless daily grinding of grain into flour to feed a large community, and, in a sense, they were already an anachronism. The infinitely more convenient water-mill was already known, but there were no suitable water-courses close to the fort. The large number of querns has been used as evidence for centralized grain-processing at Dunadd for the surrounding population, but the population of the fort itself over some three hundred years of occupation would easily require this number of hand-querns.

Most of the querns were made of local stone, but two were made of garnet-schist and must

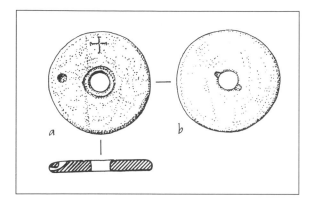

31 The cross-marked quern from Dunadd.

have been imported either from Knapdale or from the east side of Loch Fyne, the closest outcrops to Dunadd. Both were also particularly well carved compared with the other querns. One bears an incised cross with expanded triangular terminals, which is a very distinctive type and which links Dunadd with Iona (31). Six crosses of this type are known among the Iona collection of gravestones, and others are known from Tiree, in the Scoor Cave and the Nun's Cave on the south coast of the Ross of Mull, from Eileach an Naoimh in the Garvellachs, and from Barnakill near Dunadd itself. It seems possible that it was a monk from Iona who carved the cross on the quernstone, perhaps to protect the household in which the quern was used. There are two more clues

32 The stone disc inscribed 'inomine', in the name (of the Lord).

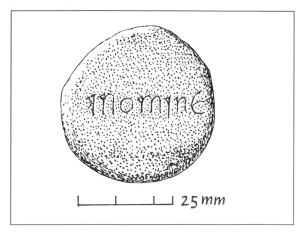

suggesting the presence of a monk, although not necessarily on the same occasion. One is a small slate disc on which the letters 'inomine' have been inscribed, as an abbreviated version of the Latin phrase *in nomine*, meaning in the name (of the Lord) (32). The other is a small piece of orpiment, a yellow sulphide of arsenic which was used as a yellow pigment in painting illuminated manuscripts, including the *Book of Kells*. It may have fallen out of a monk's satchel. Orpiment is a very rare mineral, and it would have been imported from the Mediterranean, perhaps from Vesuvius in Italy or from farther afield in Asia Minor.

The orpiment was just one minor component of the exotic goods reaching the lands around the Irish Sea in the sixth and seventh centuries. Pottery and glassware imported from the Continent reached Dunadd; indeed, Dunadd boasts the largest known collection of the hard white range of pottery made in western France (E-ware). There are also items of Anglo-Saxon origin, which may perhaps have arrived as gifts or as personal possessions of Northumbrian exiles who are known to have sought refuge in Dalriada. They include buckles and brooches, and a superb gold stud set with a deep red garnet, which was probably lost from some larger piece of aristocratic jewellery.

Fine brooches and dress-pins were also made within the fort, for there are many moulds and crucibles left behind by an accomplished bronzeworker. Designs were scratched on old roof-slates, perhaps to work out complicated interlace or as practice for an apprentice (33).

Among the range of more prosaic iron tools, carpenters' equipment bears silent witness to the many timber buildings that existed within the fort. Some impression of the potential size of the population can be gained from an Irish poem which refers to a king's entourage, including his poet, scholar, hospitaller, doctor, smith, steward, cook, engraver, fort-builder, shieldmaker and soldiers. All these people, along with their servants, had to be housed. As at Iona, the houses at Dunadd are likely to have

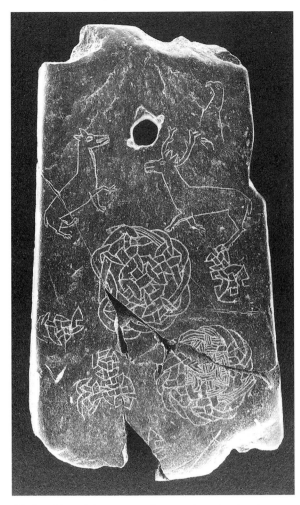

33 An old roof-slate was used to practise animal and interlace designs.

been timber-built, perhaps on stone foundations. Again the early Irish literary sources provide a welcome glimpse. A law tract dating to around 700 describes the house of a wealthy landowner: 'It is of wickerwork to the lintel ... Two doorways in it. A door for one of them, a hurdle for the other, and this without [projecting] wattles, without protuberances. A bare fence of boards around it. An oaken plank between every two beds.' It was very important that the sharp wattles should not project, for another law covers the compensation required if anyone were injured by them! Wattles were certainly used in the early monastic buildings at Iona, for Adomnán refers to Columba sending

monks 'to bring bundles of wattles ... for the building of a guesthouse' (II, 3).

A fort like Dunadd was clearly at the top end of the social and administrative scale, but its buildings and equipment were not unique. It is worth looking at two smaller residences in the vicinity of the fort and contemporary with it.

Some 7km (4.35 miles) east of Dunadd, as the crow flies, is Loch Glashan. In 1960, a crannog was discovered close to the south-east shore, and excavations revealed the remains of a large rectangular timber house dating to the seventh century. The water-logged conditions had preserved a range of wooden objects, including oblong bowls, a spoon, a bucket and a paddle, together with leather from shoes, a tunic and a sheath for a knife. As at Dunadd, there was an unusual number of querns – parts of at least thirteen rotary querns. Evidence of metalworking, a fine bronze brooch and sherds from five imported pottery vessels combine to underline the wealth of the inhabitants of the crannog.

Smaller forts in Argyll, presumably the homes of lesser warlords, also afforded a similar life-style to that at Dunadd, and some may have figured on the royal circuit. The circular fort at Ardifuir, for example, is still an impressive structure and must originally have been a splendid sight, a warlord's residence worthy of entertaining the king. It lies north-west of Dunadd, in a valley that runs down to a sheltered sandy bay. Excavations almost a hundred years ago yielded imported pottery and a stone mould and crucible similar to those at Dunadd; modern excavation would doubtless produce more such prestigious material. From the fort at Kildonan on the west coast of Kintyre has come a brooch so similar to one of the moulds from Dunadd that it may have been the work of the same craftsman. Metalworkers are likely to have been itinerant and to have travelled from one household to another, wherever there were affluent patrons. Evidence of moulds and crucibles at Kildonan suggest that a metalworker was in temporary residence at one time, perhaps the occasion when the brooch was made.

The fort at Dunollie

In the monastic annals kept at Iona, one fort is mentioned more often than any other. This is Dun Ollaigh, now Dunollie, just north of Oban. It was burned in 686 and again in 698, destroyed in 701 by Selbach, presumably as part of some power-struggle for the Dál Riata kingship, and rebuilt by him in 714. The last entry records that a Pictish warlord, Talorgan, was captured 'near the citadel of Ollaigh'. Of the known Dál Riata strongholds, Dunollie is certainly the closest to Iona, and its prominence in the Iona annals may reflect no more than that proximity, rather than that it was specially important in the kingdom in the late seventh and early eighth centuries. Nevertheless, it is likely to have been one of the power-centres in which the high king and his retinue would stay from time to time.

The visible remains on Dunollie belong to a fifteenth-century tower-house and courtyard, stronghold of the MacDougall family. It is a superb location on a rocky promontory, highly defensive and with a clear view over Oban Bay, the islands of Kerrera and Lismore, and the Sounds of Kerrera and Mull. Excavations in 1978 by Leslie and Elizabeth Alcock revealed traces of occupation in the seventh to ninth centuries, but most of this early phase had been obliterated by the later castle. The earliest structure is likely to have been a small but stout stone-walled fort set on the highest point of the hill. This would have been the fort destroyed by Selbach in 701, and the same site was used by the builders of the later tower-house. Although the fort is thus lost, excavation revealed a contemporary bronzeworker's hearth with fragments of clay moulds which show that ornamental dress-pins were one of the products commissioned by its inhabitants. When the fort was rebuilt, a rampart with a strong outer face of massive stones was erected round the vulnerable north and east sides of the rock stack.

Only 2 per cent of the summit of the stack was excavated, yet it produced a wide range of finds, including iron weapons and carpenter's tools, bronzeworking debris, bone pins and part of a comb, and a blue glass bead. There were also sherds from four pottery vessels imported from the Bordeaux area of France. These are all items appropriate to a wealthy household.

Aristocratic jewellery

Excavation of high-status secular settlements and major monasteries can usually be relied upon to yield evidence of fine metalworking. It is normally only the debris that is left, rather than the products or even the tools, but that is enough to show that wealth was spent in part on commissioning elegant brooches and pins, which would themselves, when worn, convey visually the status in society of the proud owner. Monks also wore brooches on occasion, as can be seen from depictions on carved stones and in illustrated manuscripts. A legend preserved in the *Book of Lecan* of 1416 mentions a brooch known as the Delg Aidechta (Brooch of the Testament) which was kept as a Columban relic at Iona, but, if it existed, it has not survived. Monasteries had need of other fine metalwork for the glory of God. Church plate could include dishes, strainers, ladles and chalices of bronze, silver and gold, sometimes inlaid with coloured enamel, glass or amber. Ornate reliquaries held bones, books or personal belongings of revered saints. A glimpse of the metalworking carried out in the monastery at Iona has been revealed by excavation (see pp. 41–2), but it is meagre compared with the scale of activity that is likely to have taken place there in the seventh to ninth centuries. Valuable items would also have been donated to the monastery – enough to ensure that, for the Vikings, it was worth returning to raid time and time again.

Irish brooches in Mull

Among the most tantalizing clues that the archaeologist can encounter are 'stray finds'. These are single objects that were lost or buried many centuries ago and happen to have been found again, often with no precise record of where or how they were found. All that is

34 An Irish penannular brooch from Mull.

certain about them is that they exist. But at least the archaeologist can compare them with similar artefacts and perhaps make an informed guess about where and when they were made. This is true of two brooches, said to have been found in Mull sometime before the mid-nineteenth century and now in the National Museums of Scotland. By comparison, it is possible to be reasonably certain that they were made somewhere in Ireland in the eighth century. But were they really found in Mull and not acquired in Ireland and taken to Mull by an antiquarian collector? Were their original owners wealthy residents of Mull?

The larger of the two brooches is a superb example of the metalworker's craft (**34**). It was cast in bronze with decoration in high relief and was then gilded, and there are settings for twenty-one ornamental studs. The Keeper of the Museum in Edinburgh, Joseph Anderson, writing in the late nineteenth century, evoked

the beauty of the brooch when it was fresh from the jeweller's hands: 'when the metal retained the original lustre of its surface, and the coloured settings were in their places, it must have had an appearance of gorgeous magnificence'. The triangular panels on the terminals and the curving panels on the hoop of the brooch are filled with interlaced animals, and there are more animals on the back. There are also long-snouted animal heads clasping the tops of the triangular terminals and below the rectangular plate on the pin. An intriguing detail is that there was originally a cross-bar joining the two terminals, which was later removed. The reason for this is probably that the owner of the brooch wished to have it adapted to suit the fashion in Scotland, where such brooches were made with a gap between the terminals. With a gap, it is possible to fasten the brooch more safely. The pin is passed twice through the material and then through the gap, and the hoop is then turned in such a way that the pin cannot slip back through the gap (see **34**).

The brooch is 114mm (about 4in) in diameter, and its pin is 179mm (7in) long. With the point of the pin projecting so far, a brooch like this could be quite dangerous. An early Irish law tract recognizes the danger, and states that, if a person is injured by the pin of a brooch, the wearer is not at fault if the pin does not project too far and if it is correctly worn, by men on the shoulder and by women on the breast. This seems to have been the custom in Pictland too, for the lady rider carved on the Hilton of Cadboll stone is wearing a large brooch centrally on her chest, while the three clerics on the Invergowrie stone wear theirs on their shoulders.

Iona's monks

Iona's function as a monastery was not that of a 'desert place in the ocean' but as part of the secular world. Columba himself travelled widely in Ireland, Dalriada and Pictland, and his relations with the King of Strathclyde were sufficiently close to suggest that he may well have visited parts of that British kingdom. His monks also travelled on his behalf and brought back news of the wider world. News would be brought by the many visitors to the monastery, some from as close as Mull and others from England and Ireland. In Adomnán's own time, there was a famous visitor to Iona, Bishop Arculf, who had journeyed to the Holy Land and to Rome, Constantinople and Alexandria.

Most of Columba's monks appear to have been Irishmen, but Adomnán describes two as Englishmen, one named Pilu and the other, a baker, named Genereus. The first monk to die at Iona was a Briton. Whether any of the Irishmen were of the Dál Riata is unknown, but it seems likely that, as time passed, there would be local recruits to the community, for Adomnán implies that Iona was the spiritual centre of Dalriada. Some of the early graveslabs found at the monastery record the name of the deceased monk (Maíl-Phátraic, Echoid, Fergus, Éogan, Flann, Loingsechán), but most are anonymous. One of Columba's monks was Berach, who may have been the same holy man to whom the church at Kilberry (Church of Berach) was dedicated.

Apart from ordaining Aedán mac Gabráin as King of the Dál Riata, the most telling indication of Columba's status in secular as well as ecclesiastical matters is his presence at the meeting at Druim Cett, near the Columban monastery of Derry in Ireland, between Aedán and the overlord of the Northern Uí Néill, Aed mac Ainmirech. At this time in the late sixth century the King of the Dál Riata ruled on both sides of the Irish Sea, and his overlord in the Irish homeland was a potent force in the fortunes of his people. Columba was there not only as Aedán's most important cleric but also as a close kinsman to Aed, and it is even possible that the meeting took place as a result of Columba's diplomacy. The reason for the meeting is not made clear by the historical sources, but it was probably in response to problems that had arisen on Irish soil between the Dál Riata and the Northern Uí Néill. The outcome of the meeting and the date at which it took place are even more uncertain, but the date is thought to have been around AD 590. By this time, Columba had founded monasteries in Ireland both at Derry and at Durrow, as well as lesser houses.

5
Iona, Pictland and Northumbria

In face of that unavoidable journey
No man is wiser than needs be
When reflecting, before his departure,
On what may be decided for his soul,
By way of good or evil, after his death-day.

Bede composed this verse as he lay on his death-bed in the monastery at Jarrow on 25 May 735. He was an outstanding scholar, who wrote historical and scientific works as well as hymns and poems, the latter including a *Life of St Cuthbert* in graceful Latin hexameters. His great *Historia Ecclesiastica Gentis Anglorum* (*History of the English Church and People*) was completed in 731 after many years of gathering material, and it records much of interest on the subject of Iona's relations with Pictland and his own Northumbria.

Iona and Pictland

Bede is quite clear that Columba had a mission to convert the Picts: 'In the year of our Lord 565 ... there came from Ireland a priest and abbot, outstanding in the monastic way of life, to preach the word of God to the provinces of the northern Picts, which are separated from those of the southern Picts by a range of steep and desolate mountains.' He believed that the Picts to the south of the Grampian mountains had already been converted by St Ninian of Whithorn, although the extent of Whithorn's influence is now thought not to have embraced lands beyond Fife. Certainly Dallán Forgaill,

who wrote the poem called *Amra Choluimb Chille* (*The Elegy of Colum Cille*) soon after Columba's death, refers to the saint working among the Pictish tribes along the River Tay:

> For he has died to us, the leader of nations who guarded the living,
> he has died to us, who was our chief of the needy,
> he has died to us, who was our messenger of the Lord,
> for we do not have the seer who used to keep fears from us,
> for he does not return to us, he who would explain the true Word,
> for we do not have the teacher who would teach the tribes of the Tay.

Later in the poem, Dallán writes: 'His blessing turned them, the mouths of the fierce ones who lived on the Tay, to the will of the king', which seems to imply that Columba had the authority of the Pictish king to convert his people.

Like Bede, Adomnán stresses Columba's activities among the northern Picts. There are several ways in which this apparent conflict with Dallán may be solved. Dallán's phrase 'tribes of the Tay' may not have been intended to be taken too literally but rather as a general reference to the Picts. Although Adomnán locates the Pictish king and his retinue in the Inverness area, it does not follow that the king was always based in that area, for, as we have seen, the normal practice for the king was to circulate through the kingdom. For Columba, coming from Iona, it would have been very convenient to visit the king when he was at the north end of the Great Glen, that natural route across Scotland. Even if Bridei's base was in the North, his jurisdiction is likely to have extended south to the Tay, as it did north to Orkney. And if Columba's work among the tribes of the Tay took place after Bridei's death, the political map of Pictland may have changed, and the royal seat may have been in the South.

There were certainly Columban monks in southern Pictland by the late seventh century, for established monastic communities were expelled by the Pictish king in 717, as a result of his decision to adhere to the Roman Church of Northumbria (they were to return later). Simon Taylor has drawn attention to three clusters of place-names containing the Gaelic element *cill*, meaning church, in eastern Fife, Atholl and Easter Ross, and he argues that these names represent Columban foundations. Archaeology can also offer some support for early influence from Iona in the form of small iron handbells found in Fife, Perthshire and Angus. They cannot be dated precisely, but some at least are likely to be as early as the seventh century, and they are typical artefacts of the early Irish Church.

It is often assumed that Columba converted Bridei, son of Maelchon, to Christianity, but Adomnán does not make that claim. It would have been a great coup to win over the king himself, and Adomnán would surely have recorded it as one of Columba's achievements if it had happened. He makes much of Columba's success in proving the strength of Christianity over Bridei's pagan 'magician' or priest (II, 33), and of Bridei's respect for the holy man. On Columba's 'first tiring expedition' to visit Bridei, the king ignored his arrival at the gates of the royal fortress, but Columba with God's help opened the gates, and 'from that day onwards, throughout the rest of his life, that ruler greatly honoured the holy and venerable man, as was

fitting, with high esteem' (II, 35). It is not clear from Adomnán's account how many times Columba visited Pictland, but the words 'first tiring expedition' imply that Columba made the journey to meet the king more than once, and it is likely that there were other journeys not involving the king.

Columba succeeded in converting some individual households. How many is again impossible to judge, but Adomnán mentions a family in Glen Urquhart (III, 14) and a dying Pictish soldier in Skye (I, 33), together with an unlocated but clearly wealthy household: 'At the time when St Columba passed some days in the province of the Picts, a certain layman with his whole household heard and believed the word of life, through an interpreter, at the preaching of the holy man; and believing, was baptized, the husband, with his wife and children, and his servants' (II, 32). The reference to an interpreter reflects the fact that Irish and Pictish, although branches of a common Celtic tongue, were sufficiently different to make the one unfamiliar to speakers of the other.

Occasionally Adomnán provides interesting circumstantial details. Although some may be no more than story-telling convention, the barred gates of the Pictish royal fortress and the mention of the king's house within it accord well with what is known of royal sites of this period. There are several contenders for Bridei's fort near the River Ness, including the site of the later medieval castle of Urquhart on Loch Ness, where excavation has revealed traces of Pictish occupation (35). The Iron Age hill-fort of Craig Phadrig south-west of Inverness was reused in Pictish times, although it was probably not grand enough to have been more than a fleeting bed-and-breakfast for the king. The rocky knoll of Urquhart would certainly suit the passage in Adomnán's *Life* which describes Columba setting off by boat on Loch Ness (II, 34). But, if a long-term royal base is sought, the great Pictish fort at Burghead on the south shore of the Moray Firth east of Inverness has pride of place. The largest of all known Pictish forts, this

35 A Pictish royal fortress may lie beneath Urquhart Castle on Loch Ness.

had the potential to act as springboard for naval as well as military exploits, and it seems, from the evidence of radiocarbon dating, to have been in operation throughout Pictish times.

The old soldier who died in Skye was buried beneath a cairn of stones, a tradition for which there is archaeological evidence. Low cairns with square or circular kerbs and central inhumation burials have been dated to Pictish times and associated with Pictish symbol stones; none as yet has been found in Skye, but they are concentrated in the Inverness area. This type of burial may have been used in Dalriada, perhaps while the area was still Pictish, for the low cairn on Eileach an Naoimh known as Eithne's Grave has a circular kerb. It also has an early cross-marked stone, but that may have been added later (see p. 87).

In a miracle that took place in Ireland, Adomnán mentions a Pictish monk named Éogenán, who had in his possession a book of hymns copied in Columba's handwriting (II, 9); he may therefore have belonged either to the Iona monastery or to one of its dependencies in Dalriada, Ireland or Pictland. Columba is said to have founded monasteries in Pictland as well as in Dalriada (II, 46), but unfortunately Adomnán felt it unnecessary to name them. The name that Adomnán uses for Urquhart is the Irish Airchartdan, and it has been suggested that there may have been a Columban monastery there, although no physical or documentary proof exists. Irish annals mention monasteries at St Andrews in Fife and Applecross in Wester Ross, but neither was a Columban foundation. The presence of early Christian sculpture and sometimes historical evidence implies the existence of monasteries at Tarbat in Easter Ross, Rosemarkie in the Black Isle, Kinneddar in Moray, Brechin in Angus and Abernethy on the south side of the Tay; and important lay churches with royal associations existed at Meigle in Perthshire, St Vigeans in Angus and Burghead on the coast of Moray. But none of these need be earlier than the eighth century.

Scholars often doubt whether Pictish monks were truly literate, because not one manuscript survives apart from copies of the king-list. But credit for literacy should be given at least to the major monasteries of Pictland. The king-list was in existence by AD 724 and maintained thereafter; a note in the margin of one page refers to a royal grant of land at Abernethy, which suggests not only that the list may have been compiled at Abernethy but also that, as Wendy Davies recognized, there were formal charters in use in Pictish times. There are other strong hints of literacy too, from the magnificent inscription carved on a stone at Tarbat to the historical record of a scribe working at Meigle in Perthshire (probably a cleric working for the king). Isabel Henderson has argued that some of the entries concerning events in Pictland that appear in the Irish annals may have been derived from an annal kept in the monastery at Applecross on the coast of Wester Ross, on the grounds that the Pictish name, Aporcrosan, is used. Wester Ross is likely to have remained part of Pictland until the ninth century, and the monastery at Applecross appears to have had the services of a Pictish sculptor, who carved a stone with spiral decoration very similar to that at St Vigeans in Angus (on cross-slab no. 7).

Itinerant Pictish sculptors?

Most of the larger cross-slabs and crosses of the eighth and ninth centuries must have been carved close to the place in which they were set up, simply because they were too vulnerable to damage during transportation. Good craftsmen would be in great demand and probably, like metalworkers, travelled round the country undertaking commissions wherever they were needed. This scenario assumes that they were lay workers rather than monks, although they could well have been attached to a monastery – unfortunately even the early Irish texts provide no information as to how stone-carving was organized. There were certainly schools of carving in Pictland and in Ireland, to account for close similarities between stones, and it is not difficult to envisage stonemasons being sent out, for instance, from the monasteries at Rosemarkie or Tarbat to carve the great cross-slabs at Nigg, Shandwick and Hilton of Cadboll.

Were itinerant craftsmen responsible for the early high crosses of Iona? The crosses stand in

36 The great Pictish cross-slab at Nigg in Easter Ross.

sharp contrast to the modest graveslabs; anyone handy with a chisel and hammer could have carved a simple cross on a boulder, whereas the crosses required trained sculptors. As Ian Fisher has remarked, the crosses convey the impression of being 'an early and experimental group, and not derived from any established tradition of stone-carving', and he argues for the import of 'stone-carvers who may well have been Picts'. The serpent-and-boss decoration on both St Oran's and St John's Crosses appears also in Pictish sculpture, particularly on the Nigg cross-slab (36).

Another sculptural link between Pictland and Iona lies in a form of church furniture. This is the stone shrine consisting of corner-posts, side-panels and lid (although in no case does the lid still survive). The most famous and most elaborately decorated example was found at St Andrews in Fife, but parts of others have been identified in eastern Scotland, on the Moray Firth and in Orkney and Shetland. The corner-posts are the most distinctive component because they bear longitudinal grooves into which the side-panels slot, and it is corner-posts that have survived at Iona (now in St Ronan's Museum, no. 105; 37). Each has two grooves on adjacent faces, and one has a small hollow in the top, perhaps to take the tenon of a decorative finial. They may not belong to the same shrine because one was found in Reilig Odhráin and the other in a stone-pile at the Abbey, and neither can be dated. In the reconstruction drawing (38), the front corner-posts have been given carved finials resembling the bosses covered with knitted interlace on St John's Cross. The lower ends of the corner-posts and, sometimes, the lower edges of the side-panels were sunk into the ground to give the structure stability, and their lids are in most cases likely to have been flat.

These shrines were less than a metre long and were designed to hold the bones of a saint. By the time that a saint had been canonized, and the decision had been taken to transfer his or her remains from the grave into a shrine, the

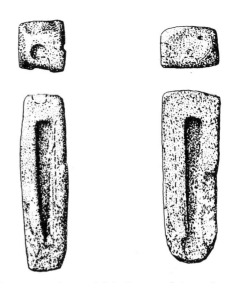

37 Corner-posts from a slab-built stone shrine at Iona.

body would normally have been reduced to disarticulated bones. The longest of these would be the leg bones, and all would fit easily into one of these shrines. An exception was St Cuthbert, whose exhumed body was found to be merely desiccated and still articulated in 698, and he therefore required a full-length wooden shrine-coffin.

The closest parallels to these Iona corner-posts are in Orkney and Shetland. One of the posts from St Ninian's Isle in Shetland is not only topped with a low ornamented knob but has arrangements of four and three small hollows decorating one side. Such motifs of grouped hollows or bosses reflect early Christian numerical symbolism, and they appear at Iona, elsewhere in Dalriada and in Pictland.

A third corner-post at Iona has an elongated stem (no. 104) and may belong to the composite base of a cross such as that in which St John's Cross stood and which had to support considerable weight. Alternatively, it could have been part of a composite corner-post shrine. It is made of imported garnet-schist, like the two special querns from Dunadd (see pp. 51–2), and it begs the question of lay patronage at Iona, which is at present difficult to evaluate.

38 Artist's reconstruction of the Iona shrine.

Northumbria

If only the Pictish Church had had a historian like the Venerable Bede, we would know more about the location of Columban monasteries in Pictland. The English Church was fortunate to have a scholar of the calibre of Bede, and, fortunately for Scotland, Bede's interests sometimes included events to the north and north-west of Northumbria. Without his account, we would know nothing from historical sources of Iona's involvement with Northumbria, although we might guess from the surviving high crosses that there had been some connection. There had been a mission from Canterbury to convert the Northumbrian kingdom to Christianity in the 620s, but it collapsed after the death in 633 of the Northumbrian king, Edwin. His successor was Oswald, already a Christian and apparently baptized in Iona, along with his younger brother and other companions. Not unnaturally,

Oswald sent envoys to Iona to request a spiritual leader for his kingdom. The first candidate was unsuccessful and history does not even record his name. According to Bede, he was a man of 'austere disposition', to whom the English refused to listen and for whom the English were 'an uncivilized people of an obstinate and barbarous temperament'. But Iona was still aware of its responsibilities in Northumbria, and the monk Aidan suggested that the way to approach the conversion of the English was to give them 'the milk of simpler teaching' and gradually to introduce them to the word of God. Bede records that Aidan was recognized as 'a fit person to be made bishop and to be sent to instruct the ignorant and unbelieving, since he was particularly endowed with the grace of discretion, the mother of virtues'. Thus Aidan was made a bishop and sent from Iona on a missionary expedition to Northumbria.

Aidan founded a monastery in Lindisfarne in 635. This is a small tidal island almost 2km (1.24

miles) off the coast of Northumbria, one of a group of islands known as the Farne Islands, from which the contemporary royal fort of Bamburgh would have been visible along the coast to the south. The island situation was thus similar to that of Iona, except that here the island was accessible on foot and on horseback at low tide. As in Iona, the monastery was built behind an ancient raised beach, which may have acted as part of the boundary of the monastic enclosure, but at Lindisfarne there are no surviving traces of the vallum. Very few remains of the early monastery have been found, for the same site was used, again as at Iona, for a Benedictine monastery in the twelfth century. Even amongst the substantial collection of Anglo-Saxon stone-carving at Lindisfarne, there is nothing that need be dated earlier than the eighth century.

> When Bishop Aidan departed this life, he was succeeded in the bishopric by Finan, who had been consecrated and sent by the Scots. He built a church in the Isle of Lindisfarne, his see, constructing it not of stone, but of hewn oak thatched with reeds after the Scots manner.

This famous passage from Bede's *History* explains in one sentence why traces of early churches are so difficult to find in north Britain. They were built of timber, which rots away, and, where they were subsequently replaced by stone-built churches on the same spot, the chances of finding any evidence of an earlier wooden structure are remote. But being timber-built need not imply that they were unsophisticated. Contemporary timber halls in secular contexts in Britain and Ireland could be very impressive, and the timber stave-built churches that survive today in Scandinavia from the eleventh century demonstrate the possibilities with skilled carpenters at work.

A daughter house of Lindisfarne was founded by Aidan at Melrose (now Old Melrose) beside the River Tweed in southern Scotland. This was shortly before 650, and Northumbrian control at that time extended north to the Firth of Forth.

The monastic vallum can still be seen at Old Melrose, cutting off a promontory of land formed by a great meander of the river (the Cistercian monastery was founded farther west in 1136). It was at Melrose that Cuthbert entered the Church in 651, rising fast to become Prior of Melrose and in 664 Prior of Lindisfarne. For thirty years from about 655, southern Pictland was under Northumbrian domination, until the Northumbrian king Ecgfrith and his army were vanquished by the Picts at the battle of Nechtansmere, near Dunnichen in Angus, in 685. A Northumbrian monastery had been established at Abercorn on the south side of the Firth of Forth, but its bishop, Trumwine, decided after the defeat at Nechtansmere that discretion was indeed the better part of valour, and he and his monks abandoned Abercorn.

But it was in the context of such ecclesiastical contacts between Northumbria and Pictland that the creation of the superb Pictish cross-slabs must be seen. One of the earliest and most sublime was at Aberlemno, near the battlefield of Nechtansmere (39). The animal decoration in the background to the cross links this masterpiece of stone-carving with the *Lindisfarne Gospels*, an illustrated book created at Lindisfarne in the first quarter of the eighth century, and with sculpture at the Northumbrian monastery of Monkwearmouth at the same period.

The Easter controversy

Bishop Finan of Lindisfarne became embroiled in a long-standing and far-reaching controversy over the date of Easter, which was eventually to involve Adomnán himself. The date depended upon arithmetic calculations of both the lunar and the solar calendars, and it was the subject of hot debate within the Christian Church in Britain from the sixth century into the eighth. The Irish Church adhered to one system of reckoning and the English, following the Roman Church, to another. Lindisfarne adhered to its inherited Iona tradition under both Finan and his successor, Colman, but a synod (a meeting of Church leaders) held at Whitby in 664 brought matters to

39 Pictish cross-slab in the churchyard at Aberlemno in Angus.

a head and decreed that the Roman view was correct. Another fifty years were to pass before that decision was accepted by the king in Pictland and even longer before it was accepted by the Columban church in Iona and elsewhere. Involved in the dispute was not just the date of Easter but also the correct way for monks to wear the tonsure, the hair-cut that, along with their robes, distinguished monks from laymen. The Roman way was to shave the crown of the head and the back and sides to leave a ring of hair, whereas the Celtic tradition was to shave away the hair at the front of the head as well, leaving an arc of hair round the back of the head.

Adomnán paid two visits to Northumbria while he was Abbot of Iona. He was already friendly with King Aldfrith, who had previously spent some time at Iona, and was a welcome guest at the Northumbrian royal court in 685–6 and 687–8. It is not recorded whether he visited Lindisfarne or met St Cuthbert, but both seem

likely; Cuthbert was in residence as bishop at Lindisfarne at the time of Adomnán's first visit to Northumbria, although he was at his hermitage on Farne at the time of his death on 20 March 687. As a result of his first-hand experience of the Roman way of reckoning the date of Easter, Adomnán seems to have been won over, but not apparently into accepting the Roman tonsure as well. In the matter of Easter, his community in Iona was reluctant to follow suit and held out against the Roman way until twelve years after his death.

Adomnán as a scholar

Bede described Adomnán as 'a good and wise man with an excellent knowledge of the scriptures'. After Columba, he was Iona's most famous abbot, not simply for writing the *Life of Columba* but also for a humane Law of Innocents (**40**). Enacted at Birr, some 40km (25 miles) from Durrow in Ireland, in 697, this was a law that emanated from the Church but could be enforced over both ecclesiastical and lay communities. Its object was to protect the 'innocents', that is clergy, women and children, from injury. Among those whom Adomnán persuaded to support the law were not only churchmen and kings from all over Ireland and Dalriada but also the Pictish king, which provides a rare insight into diplomatic relations with the Picts. It may be doubted whether the Pictish king attended the assembly at Birr in person, but he may well have sent an envoy, probably a cleric from a Pictish monastery.

Adomnán also wrote *De Locis Sanctis* (*On the Holy Places*) from notes that he made while listening to the much-travelled Bishop Arculf, who had spent three years in the Holy Land, Rome, Alexandria and Constantinople. He added much that was derived from his own understanding of the Bible, and in medieval times this book was considered more important than the *Life of St Columba*, itself the best of contemporary hagiography. In his preface, Adomnán explains that he wrote at the time on wax tablets and later transferred the work on to

1 The Bay at the Back of the Ocean.

2 The fort on Dùn Bhuirg.

3 Iona from the air, with St Ronan's Bay and the village,
the Abbey to the right and Dùn I beyond.

4 The village at St Ronan's Bay.

5 Iona Abbey against the hills of Mull.

6 Iona Abbey from the air, showing the monastic enclosure, the Mill Stream and the straight embankment of Iomaire Tochair.

7 St Martin's Cross, with Tòrr an Aba beyond.

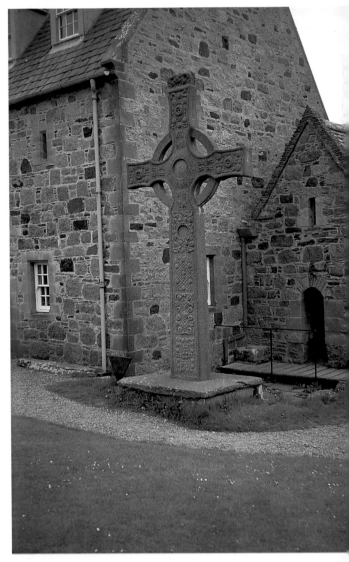

8 The replica of St John's Cross stands in front of
St Columba's Oratory.

9 The Kildalton Cross, Islay.

10 The cliffs of Canna from the air, with the circular enclosure of Sgòr nam Ban-naomha.

11 The Nunnery, Iona.

12 MacLean's Cross.

40 The monastery at Iona in Adomnán's time was a place of scholarly learning; this artist's impression shows the saint on Tòrr an Aba receiving a report of a church newly built overseas. The stone building behind is modelled on an Irish oratory.

parchment. A tablet is also mentioned in passing in the *Life of Columba* (I, 35) and in many other saints' *Lives* by various authors, and it is clear that wax tablets were the normal medium for short-term writing and for training novices in the art of calligraphy. They could be single tablets or several tied together like an unwieldy book. A beautifully preserved example of the latter can be seen in the National Museum of Ireland in Dublin; known as the Springmount Bog tablets, these are six boards of yew, each 210 by 77mm (about 8 by 3in), tied together with a leather thong. Each of the four inner leaves is hollowed out on both sides to hold a layer of beeswax, and each of the outer leaves is hollowed only on its inner surface, and thus, when the tablets are closed, all the wax surfaces are protected (and indeed the writing still survives).

Literacy at Iona

An Iona *Chronicle* is known to have existed because it was copied and incorporated into the Irish *Annals of Ulster*. It appears to have been written from at least the early seventh century to about AD 740, and it recorded information about the deaths of abbots at Iona, about political events in Dalriada and Pictland, and about journeys between Iona and Ireland. Apart from Adomnán's own writings, there exists also a body of poetry written in Irish and Latin by monks at Iona. Thanks to Thomas Owen Clancy and Gilbert Márkus, these poems are now easily accessible both in the original and in translation, and they include some fine and moving pieces. Not every monastery had a scriptorium, but the importance of Iona and the scale of its literary output suggest that a proper communal writing-room and library must have existed there.

In the *Life*, Adomnán mentions Columba's writing-hut and other monks' working-huts, but he does not specifically mention a communal scriptorium. Twice he refers to *scrinia*, coffers or book-chests, in contexts that imply their use

65

41 A detail from the *Book of Kells*: a horse and rider have been painted between two lines of script.

at Iona, but these could have been kept in the side-room of the church. It may be that, in the early days of the monastery, monks wrote in individual huts, but that in time a communal scriptorium was built, properly lit to allow the creation of the minute detail of illustrated manuscripts. Analysis of the works written at Iona allows a glimpse of the contents of the library available to the monks, because other authors are often quoted. Aside from the Bible itself, the library probably contained a number of early works including Jerome's commentaries on the Bible and *De Civitate Dei* (*On the City of God*) by Augustine of Hippo, and other famous books were added as the years went by, such as Pope Gregory the Great's *Dialogues*.

Books written in Columba's own hand became holy relics, although the only surviving manuscript that may have been the work of the saint is the *Cathach of St Columba*, a book of psalms which was enshrined in a silver casket in the eleventh century, more than 400 years after it was written. There are good reasons to believe that two of the most beautiful illuminated gospel-books that survive today were created or at least begun at Iona: the *Book of Durrow*, which was written and painted in the second half of the seventh century, in Adomnán's time, and the *Book of Kells*, which was created in the late eighth or early ninth century (**41**). These books are named after the great Irish monasteries of Durrow and Kells, in which they were later kept. Both monasteries were founded from Iona, Durrow by Columba in the late 580s and Kells by the Columban community of Iona in 807.

6
The sculpture of Iona

One of the glories of Iona today is the stone-carving that survives from the early monastery, particularly the high crosses of St Oran, St John, St Matthew and St Martin. These crosses are testimony to the wealthy patronage available to the monastery in the eighth and ninth centuries, and their art and craftsmanship are a valuable indication of the cultural links between Iona and the outside world. Françoise Henry described the decoration on the crosses as 'a turbulent and restless art begging all the time for effects of light and shade'. Even the humble and normally anonymous gravestones of the Columban monks shed light on the character of the community. The numbers used here to identify the carved stones are those used by the Royal Commission on the Ancient and Historical Monuments of Scotland in the *Iona Inventory*; although the original numbering in the Abbey and Nunnery museums was different, the conservation project now underway will include a catalogue based on the Royal Commission numbering (the latter has the advantage of reflecting the chronological and typological sequence of the stones).

It is interesting to compare the stone-carving of Iona with that of the monastery founded from Iona by Aidan at Lindisfarne in Northumbria. At Lindisfarne, a distinct house-style developed, marked by small cross-slabs with rounded tops and lettering that echoes the display script used in the illustrated manuscript known as the *Lindisfarne Gospels*. In contrast, few of Iona's gravestones bear inscriptions, and the only 'house-style' is the use of rounded boulders for the so-called pillow-stone type of grave-marker, based on the stone pillow said to have been favoured by Columba (**42**). On the other hand, whereas Iona in the mid-eighth century began to produce free-standing high crosses, Lindisfarne has only fragments of such crosses, mostly of later date and none of high quality. The unknown factor is, of course, the wooden cross, which does not survive but which could fill the gaps in any sequence. Excavations in water-logged levels in Dublin have yielded a large and elaborately carved wooden boss, which probably decorated a wooden high cross.

A stone high cross is recorded in later sources to have been set up at Lindisfarne around AD 740, in honour of St Cuthbert, and it is perhaps surprising that none is recorded at Iona in honour of either Columba or Adomnán. But the designations of Iona's surviving high crosses are neither as certain nor recorded as early as one might wish. The existence of a cross named after St Martin is recorded in 1699, and crosses named after St John and St Matthew in 1773, while the designation of St Oran's Cross was suggested in modern times by the scholar Robert Stevenson on the grounds that it was found in St Oran's Chapel. Any of these crosses could originally have been set up in honour of St Columba or St Adomnán, and there are also cross-bases lacking their crosses, which might have been similarly dedicated. According to

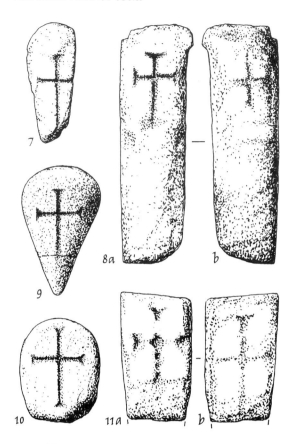

42 Boulders with incised linear crosses.

shallow groove marking out part of a circle, 1.15m (3ft 9in) in diameter (**43**). The early monastery thus appears to have had its own mill, the first, perhaps, of several built over the centuries along the Mill Stream (pp. 19–20).

Mills powered by water-driven wheels set horizontally rather than vertically are known to have been in use in Ireland from at least as early as the sixth century AD. They were built of timber with wooden wheels, and remains have been preserved in peat bogs. Any of the Irish monks of Iona could have brought the technology to the island and built a mill for the monastery.

The high crosses

Of the four surviving high crosses, St Martin's is by far the best preserved; indeed it is the only intact cross and the sole example still in its original position. In terms of design and

tradition, a long-vanished 'St Adomnán's Cross' once stood close to Port a' Chroisein (Port of the Little Cross) in what is now the northern part of the village.

In his *Life of Columba*, Adomnán refers to three crosses that were set up in the seventh century to commemorate incidents associated with the saint (I, 45 and III, 23), but these would either have been simple cross-marked stone pillars or crosses made of wood. One was set up to mark the spot at which Columba had rested on his way back to the monastery on the day of his death. Adomnán records that this cross 'was later fixed in a mill-stone' (III, 23). This is most likely to have been a wooden cross which, by Adomnán's time, had been set in one of the grinding stones from a small corn-mill. Part of the box-like base for St John's Cross is a stone which appears first to have been selected for use as a millstone; on its upper face is a

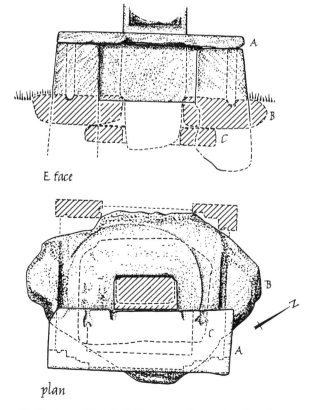

43 The base of St John's Cross: east face and projected section, and plan.

structure, St Oran's is thought to be the earliest, followed by St John's and St Martin's, but all three are dated within the mid- to late eighth century. After a gap of perhaps a century, St Matthew's Cross was carved in the ninth or even tenth century, to judge by similar crosses in Ireland. But the apparent gap may have been filled by crosses which no longer exist, such as that which once stood in the massive block of pink granite from the Ross of Mull to be seen in Reilig Odhráin (44). The socket is only 0.32m (1ft) deep, which suggests that this may have been the basal component in a box-type support such as that used for St John's Cross. The location of this boulder, 15m (49ft) south of St Oran's Chapel, may have been related to an entrance through the early vallum. High crosses could be set up at various points around a monastery, including the entrance through the monastic enclosure. Parts of four other cross-bases may be seen in the Abbey museum, including two that were also found in Reilig Odhráin (nos 99, which is part of the lid of a box-type base, and 101, a corner of a solid base) and one discovered during excavations to the south of St Columba's Shrine (no. 100, another corner of a solid base). The provenance of the fourth is unknown (no. 102, a slab with a narrow slot).

The surviving fragments of St Oran's Cross were found in St Oran's Chapel in the nineteenth century. This suggests that the cross may originally have stood in the area that became Reilig Odhráin. The solid cross-base (no. 103) still located in Reilig Odhráin is unlikely to have held this cross, however, for its slot is considerably larger than the shaft of the cross. There may thus have been two high crosses in this area, perhaps beside the main entrance into the monastic enclosure. The upper part of a plain cross-shaft (no. 81) was also found in Reilig Odhráin. St John's, St Matthew's and St Martin's Crosses all stood close to the west end of the Abbey church, and their location indicates that the original church is likely to have been in the same place as the

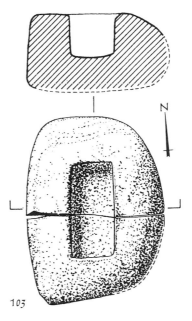

44 Solid cross-base in Reilig Odhráin.

twelfth-century church. St Martin's Cross stands proudly still in its original solid base. The replica of St John's Cross stands in the original box-type of base, close to the small oratory known as St Columba's Shrine, and the solid base of St Matthew's Cross remains in place nearby. The base of a later medieval high cross was found during excavations beside the Street of the Dead. The fragmentary remains of St Oran's, St John's and St Matthew's Crosses are displayed in the Abbey museum.

St Oran's Cross
(no. 80, mid–later eighth century)

This cross survives as fragments, and more remains of the decoration of the front of the cross than of the back. It was made of coarse mica-schist from the Ross of Mull, which is not an ideal medium for fine carving, but the craftsman was nevertheless able to create detailed and intricate decoration. The cross was designed as three pieces which fitted together with mortice-and-tenon joints: the shaft has a projecting tenon which fits into a slot or mortice in the underside of the horizontal arms (the transom) of the cross, and another slot on the

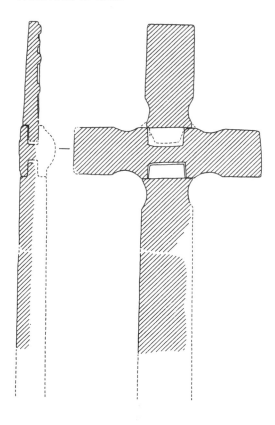

45 The mortise-and-tenon construction of St Oran's Cross.

upper side of the transom receives a tenon on the bottom of the upper arm of the cross (**45**). Only the upper part of the shaft has survived, with the result that the original height of the cross is unknown, but the arms have a span of 1.99m (6ft 6in); there are circular 'armpits' but no ring linking the arms. Much of the decoration consists of variations on the theme of raised bosses and serpents, including 'bird's-nest' bosses in which the hollow centre contains one or three smaller bosses or 'eggs'. At the top of the shaft, just below the transom, there is a carving of the Virgin and Child between two angels, which is very similar to a painting in the *Book of Kells*. It also links the cross with those at Kildalton in Islay and Drumcliff in County Sligo in Ireland. On the front of the left arm of St Oran's Cross is a scene with a human figure and a beast, which is most likely to represent either David or Daniel with a lion, although it could be Jerome removing a thorn from a lion's

paw. On the back of the cross, there are human figures carved on the horizontal arms, including a seated figure playing a harp (**46**).

St John's Cross
(no. 82, mid–later eighth century)

St John's Cross is the most intriguing of Iona's high crosses, and its history makes a sorry tale. This was a magnificent but structurally flawed creation, and it is thought likely that it fell soon after it was first set up. The problem lay in the great span and weight of its arms. With a span of almost 2.2m (7ft 3in), it is one of the two widest-known crosses in the British Isles (the other is at Ray in County Donegal). Certainly its recent history has demonstrated how vulnerable the cross was to strong winds. It was stuck together with concrete and re-erected in 1927, but a gale felled it in 1951. It was re-erected again in 1954, only to be blown down three years later. The decision was then taken to house the precious fragments indoors, and in 1970 a replica in pre-stressed concrete was set up in the original cross-base, anchored at its foot by high tensile wires to ensure stability (**colour plate 8**). The fragments of the original cross were carefully conserved by Historic Scotland, and, reconstructed on a frame, the cross was erected on behalf of the Iona Cathedral Trust in the refurbished Abbey museum on 5 September 1990 (**47**). The slots in the sides of the shaft were cut to take metal clamps in the 1950s restoration of the cross.

Meticulous study of the surviving fragments has demonstrated that the form of this cross was modified in antiquity, in an effort to make it more stable. Originally it was a ringless cross, at least 5.3m (about 17ft) tall, consisting of four separate pieces with mortice-and-tenon joints: the shaft, the lower arm (now missing), the horizontal arms and upper arm carved in one piece, and a finial at the top of the upper arm. After an early fall had proved this to be an inefficient and unstable design in a cross of this size, four curving segments were added between the arms to support their weight, thus

46 The front of St Oran's Cross.

47 The west face of St John's Cross in the Abbey museum.

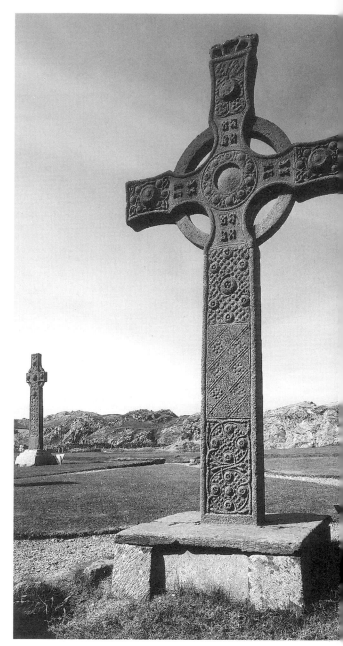

48 The east face of the modern replica of St John's Cross, with St Martin's Cross in the background.

converting the cross into its present ringed form. The shaft and cross-head are made of greenish-grey chlorite-schist from Mid Argyll, probably from the Loch Sween area, whereas the finial and the one surviving fragment of the ring are of mica-schist from the Ross of Mull. Transporting the great slabs of chlorite-schist over a distance

of some 75km (46 miles) was no mean task, but this was a far superior stone for carving to the local rocks.

The cross stood in a composite box-base consisting of four corner-posts with four linking side-slabs and a two-piece cover-slab, with two lower socket-stones, one of which was originally marked out as a millstone (see above). The western half of the cover-slab is missing, but it was replaced by a modern slab when the replica cross was erected. The socket-stones were not needed for the replica and can now be seen separately.

The decoration on St John's Cross is similar to that on St Oran's but develops the themes further. There are panels of snake-and-boss designs and 'bird's-nest' bosses, and spiral work very similar to that on the *chi–rho* page in the *Book of Kells*. At the centre of the cross-head on the east face is a massive boss, decorated with interlace and surrounded by a border of smaller bosses (**48**). The equivalent position on the west face is occupied by a circular recess designed to take a large metal boss (**49**). Unfortunately this does not survive, but it was probably made of bronze and may have been gilded and even studded with jewelled insets. There may have been another metal boss filling the circular recess in the top panel of the cross-shaft on the same face. The only figural decoration on the cross is on the finial, and it is now very damaged; it appears to show two figures, perhaps Jacob wrestling with the angel, flanked by animals.

St Martin's Cross
(no. 83, mid–later eighth century)

Still standing where monks passed it twelve hundred years ago, St Martin's Cross is a direct link with the early monastery. It is a ringed cross, 4.3m (14ft) high above its solid rectangular base of Ross of Mull granite, and it was carved from a single slab of grey epidiorite from the mainland of Argyll. Its span is only 1.19m (3ft 11in), and its side-arms barely project beyond the ring, but slots in the ends of the arms suggest that they were embellished with decorative metal panels. There are slight and tantalizing traces of an inscription in the basal panel on the west face, placed where it could be read by worshippers on their knees. The inscription is now illegible, but it may have recorded the name of the person for whom or

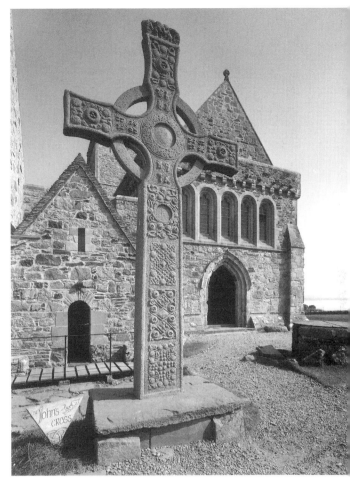

49 The modern replica of St John's Cross in front of St Columba's Shrine and the medieval Abbey church.

by whom the cross was set up. Inscriptions are relatively common on Irish and English crosses, and most do no more than request a prayer for the patron for whom the cross was set up; one at Kells dedicates the cross to Patrick and Columba.

The sculptor placed a representation of the Virgin and Child in the centre of the west face of the cross-head, and on the shaft below are carved four other scenes with figures (**50**). At the top is a cloaked Daniel flanked by lions, above Abraham poised with sword to sacrifice Isaac. Next comes David playing his harp and accompanied by another musician with triple pipes. The lowest scene shows four figures who are difficult to identify, but Isabel Henderson

73

50 The west face of St Martin's Cross.

has suggested that they represent David killing Goliath, and David before Saul. The arms of the cross are carved with animals. The east face is entirely covered with bosses and serpents, including a very large central boss, but there are no 'bird's nest' bosses (**51**).

St Matthew's Cross
(no. 84, ninth–early tenth century)

Like St Martin's Cross, St Matthew's Cross stood in a solid base of Ross of Mull granite, shaped into a stepped profile. There was clearly no demand in Dalriada for the highly ornate bases popular both in Ireland and in Northumbria. All that survives of the cross itself is part of the shaft and a fragment of arm and cross-head, but it is enough to show that this was a monolithic cross, ringed but with unpierced armpits. It was made of coarse grey sandstone, which may have been imported from the island of Colonsay. The shaft was moved into the Abbey museum in 1994. The east face bears an Adam and Eve scene above a panel of diagonal key-ornament, while the west face displays a panel of circular knotwork below a much-damaged figural scene (**52**). The Adam and Eve depiction is similar to one on the Broken Cross at Kells, where the monastery was founded from Iona in the early ninth century.

The Iona school of high crosses

Whoever commissioned these crosses will never be known, but Iona certainly had powerful and wealthy patrons. At least two Irish kings retired to Iona as monks in the second half of the eighth century. The three eighth-century crosses, St Oran's, St John's and St Martin's, have much in common in terms of decoration with the contemporary *Book of Kells*, and Ian Fisher has suggested that the inspiration for the creation of both the crosses and the great gospel-book was the enshrinement of Columba's relics in the mid-eighth century. Much has been written about the art and iconography of Iona's high crosses,

particularly about their construction, their relationships with their Irish counterparts and with the *Book of Kells*, and the links with the contemporary sculpture of Northumbria and Pictland. It is agreed that the structural design of the crosses was derived from carpentry techniques, and the wooden artefacts found in

51 The east face of St Martin's Cross.

52 Reconstruction of St Matthew's Cross with the Adam and Eve scene on the east face.

monastery at Kildalton, and the cross may be seen as a wayside prayer-cross set up by some local magnate. The ruined church beside the cross is no earlier in date than the late twelfth century, and, although three simple cross-slabs have been found, there is no reason to connect them with a church as early as the cross itself. Both the cross, carved in one piece, and its base-slab are made of local epidiorite, which is an intractable stone to carve, yet the quality and detail of this cross are superb. The cross stands 2.65m (8ft 8in) above its base, and its arms reach a span of 1.32m (4ft 4in) (**colour plate 9**). Its proportions are similar to those of St John's Cross, but its decoration is closer to that of St Martin's Cross. Both faces display wonderful variations on the serpent-and-boss theme, carved in high relief. The central roundel on the west face is flanked by lions, two of which are engagingly depicted from above, their limbs and tails entwined with serpents and other animals (**53**). As on St Martin's Cross, the east face is dominated by figural scenes, including, at the

the monastery ditch support the high level of carpentry practised from the seventh century. Douglas MacLean has claimed that 'architects built crosses' and that their decoration was carried out by craftsmen who were equally at home working either in wood or stone. The art of the crosses links the stone-carvers' expertise with that of the painters of illustrated manuscripts and with that of metalworkers, and there is every likelihood that sculpture was itself painted as well as embellished on occasion with metal bosses and plates.

St Martin's Cross is very similar in construction and decoration to the high cross at Kildalton in Islay, and it is likely that the same craftsmen were involved. There is no trace of a

53 The west face of the Kildalton Cross on Islay.

54 The east face of the Kildalton Cross.

top of the shaft, a rendering of the Virgin and
Child with angels which is very close to that on
St Oran's Cross (54). Other scenes show, on the

top arm, David and the lion, on the right arm
Abraham's sacrifice of Isaac, and on the left
Cain slaying Abel.

The snake ornament that is such a feature of
the Iona crosses and of the *Book of Kells* is

highly symbolic. One aspect of its symbolism is concerned with the fall from grace of Adam and Eve, but another is more positive, a symbol of eternity. For the snake sheds its skin and is reborn. The snake is thus a symbol of the Resurrection of Christ. Snake-and-boss designs are also a strong feature in Pictish sculpture of the late eighth and early ninth centuries, but the nature of the connection between Pictish cross-slabs and Iona crosses is not yet clear.

The latest in this small group of crosses of the Iona school stands at Keills in Knapdale. Again this is a site at which the parish church was established in the twelfth century, but the high cross dates to the late eighth or early ninth century on the grounds of its large-scale key-ornament (55). Prior to being taken into the shelter of the church in 1979, it stood on a terrace nearby.

There are six other slabs of Early Christian date, but no contemporary structures survive. The cross may have served as a focus of worship for the lay population of the area, guided by monks from Eilean Mór (see pp. 88–9).

Iona's graveslabs

High crosses were public monuments, and every monastery had its individual personal memorials marking the graves of members of its community and laymen. Those at Iona are remarkable for the number surviving and for their simplicity. There are about eighty grave-markers, including the so-called pillow-stones, upright cross-slabs and recumbent graveslabs. Even this relatively large number cannot account for all the monks buried over some three hundred years; there are probably many more stones still hidden in the soil. It is also likely that many graves were marked by wooden memorials. Most of the surviving stones are impossible to date precisely, but the collection ranges from the sixth century into later medieval times. The types of crosses carved on them also vary widely, from simple incised linear and

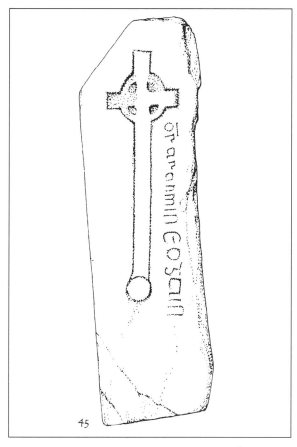

56 Graveslab inscribed 'A prayer for the soul of Éogan'.

outline crosses to sunken crosses, crosses carved in relief, crosses with expanded terminals, interlaced crosses, crosses with rings and crosses without rings. A few bear brief inscriptions written in Old Irish, such as 'A prayer for Maíl-Phátraic' (no. 14), 'A prayer for Fergus' (no. 31) and 'A prayer for the soul of Éogan' (no. 45; 56). These are useful in providing names for some of the monks, but they are so rare as to imply that personal commemoration was unimportant throughout the history of the early monastery. One beautifully carved pillow-stone bears a *chi–rho* monogram in the form of an outline cross, compass-drawn with expanded arms, with the *rho* hanging like a hook from the upper arm (no. 22; 57). The *chi–rho* symbol developed in very early Christian times in the Mediterranean as an abbreviation of the Greek name for Christ. The first two Greek letters of

Christos are called *chi* (χ) and *rho* (ρ), the capital forms of which are X and P; joined together, these became a cross with a hook at the top. Along the top edge of the stone is a Latin inscription reading 'Lapis Echodi', 'The stone of Echodius', or Echoid, as the monk would have been known in Old Irish. One of the larger recumbent graveslabs bears a very fine interlaced cross with expanded terminals within a plain border (no. 68), which was copied less successfully for a Scandinavian-speaker with a runic inscription in the border (no. 69; see pp. 96–7).

After the heyday of the high crosses, less ambitious free-standing crosses of Irish type continued to be carved at Iona in the tenth and eleventh and perhaps into the twelfth century, and there is one shaft carved in Scandinavian style which will be discussed in Chapter 8.

Occasionally Ionan rocks were used for early grave-markers. The Torridonian flagstones from the beach near the monastery provided flat slabs and boulders, and glacial boulders of dolerite and granite were used for pillow-stones. In most cases, however, slabs of more tractable mica-schist or sandstone were imported from the Ross of Mull. Many gravestones were found in Reilig Odhráin, but many others have been found in the course of work around the Abbey or have been lying around for so long that their place of discovery is now unknown. Some come from farther afield, such as the pillow-stone found near Cladh an Dìsirt (no. 60) or the cross-slab reused as a step at Sithean farm (no. 37). Several were incorporated into paving in front of St Columba's Shrine. The problem is that graveslabs are portable as well as handy for other purposes, and it is simply not possible to locate the monastic graveyard prior to Reilig Odhráin.

None of the stones has been found in modern times in association with a burial, but the very simplicity of the grave-markers suggests that the burial rites were also minimal. Even Columba, whose body lay in his cell while 'For three days and three nights the funeral rituals befitting one

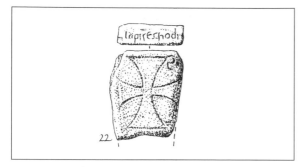

57 Grave-marker inscribed 'Lapis Echodi'.

of his honour and status were duly carried out', was then buried 'wrapped in pure linen' apparently in a simple grave-pit marked only by the stone that had been his pillow in life (III, 23). Such burials were the norm at this period, although the pit could be lined with stone slabs (known to archaeologists as a long cist); the grave would be orientated east–west, and there were rarely any artefacts placed in the grave, apart from the occasional bronze pin there to fasten the shroud. As time went on, wooden coffins became popular, and there is literary evidence for the use of a log-coffin at Iona. A log-coffin, like a logboat, consisted of a hollowed section of tree-trunk. The *Life of Adomnán*, written in the tenth century, includes verses attributed to Adomnán himself, and they describe the burial in Iona in a log-coffin of a Pictish king, Bruide mac Bile, in the late seventh century.

> It is strange,
> after ruling a kingdom:
> a small ruined hollow of oak
> about the son of Dumbarton's king.

The same *Life* attributes this verse also to Adomnán:

> If I be destined to die in Iona,
> it were a merciful leavetaking.
> I know not under the blue sky
> a better little spot for death.

7
Iona's monastic neighbours

The monastery of Iona dominates the modern perception of the early Church in Argyll and the Hebrides, but the contemporary view, certainly in the sixth century, may have been somewhat different. The survival of Adomnán's *Life of Columba* has ensured that much is known of Columba and of Iona, but other Irish monks also founded monasteries and became saints. Less is known of them, but they may have been as instrumental as Iona in converting the local lay population, even if they did not operate on as wide a stage as Iona. St Moluag founded a monastery on Lismore, St Donnan on Eigg and, in the seventh century, St Maelrubha at Applecross. The leaders of other ecclesiastical communities remain anonymous, although Eileach an Naoimh is associated by tradition with St Brendan. Church dedications can be of later date and may not be an accurate guide to the founder.

The size and function of these early church-sites vary greatly, and Iona by the eighth century was undoubtedly the largest monastery. Among the sites known from fieldwork, there are smaller monasteries and even smaller hermitages, and caves used as hermitages, as well as churches and burial-grounds for the lay population.

Monasteries

In the late twelfth century, the cathedral church of the diocese of Argyll stood on the island of Lismore. It replaced a monastery founded in the sixth century by Moluag, an Irish monk thought to have originated at Bangor in County Down, who was a contemporary of Columba and who died in AD 592. It is not known whether the early monastery was still functioning in the twelfth century, but the survival of St Moluag's crozier suggests that there was at least an active church on the site. The crozier, known as the *Bachall Mór*, became a hereditary relic and is still kept on the island by the Livingstone family. New light has been shed on the choice of Lismore for Moluag's monastery by the discovery on the island of a superb piece of Celtic finery. This is a bronze armlet of a type that was fashionable in eastern Scotland, particularly in Aberdeenshire, in the first and second centuries AD. It would have been worn by someone of wealth and high status, perhaps a Caledonian woman who came to Lismore to marry the local Celtic chief. It suggests that Lismore may have been a power-centre in Iron Age times. If so, land for St Moluag's monastery may have been granted by a secular power, and the importance of Lismore was later perpetuated by its choice for the medieval cathedral of Argyll.

The choir of the medieval church has been restored as the parish church. Nothing survives of St Moluag's Church, but the line of the monastic enclosure is thought to be reflected by the field-boundaries to the north, east and south of the existing church. They suggest a roughly circular enclosure about 240m (789ft) across, broadly equivalent to the size envisaged for Columba's monastic enclosure at Iona.

Perhaps a little smaller was St Blane's monastery at Kingarth at the south end of the island of Bute, but here some interesting structures survive. A rocky cliff acts as the west side of an oval enclosure, with a stone wall, restored in the nineteenth century, round the other sides. A twelfth-century church and graveyard occupy much of the interior, probably on the same spot as the original church. There are foundations of buildings along the foot of the scarp, some of which may be early in date. The most extraordinary is a large circular building, about 10m (32ft) across, with a very thick wall (2.5m/8ft 2in) and a single entrance – popularly known as 'The Cauldron'. This looks more like a prehistoric house than a monastic building, but it may have been reused in later times. Excavations in 1896 yielded several pieces of slate with sketches cut into them, including one with a panel of interlace alongside an initial letter, perhaps the work of a monk learning the art of illustrating manuscripts. Some of the slates are reused roof-slates, which suggests the presence of substantial buildings. St Blane is thought to have been born in Bute in AD 565 and to have been trained in this monastery; the medieval church was later dedicated to him. There are historical records of two bishops of Kingarth in the seventh century and three abbots in the following century.

St Donnan's monastery on the island of Eigg survives only in the form of early cross-slabs and the place-name, Kildonnan, although the medieval church here is likely to be located in the same place as the earlier monastery. Donnan and his fellow monks were killed in AD 617. An Irish annal records 'the burning of Donnan of Eigg on 17 April with 150 martyrs'; the number suggests a very large monastery, but there is some conflict with another source, the *Book of Leinster*, which gives the figure of fifty-four. According to the latter source, the attackers were hired by a local landowner in retaliation for loss of grazing land. But the monastery survived at least into the mid-seventh century, which is proved by documentary references to its monks, and probably longer. There was Viking activity in Eigg, including burials close to the monastic site, and a beautifully decorated sword-hilt and part of a boat have been found there. The Vikings may well have been attracted to the island in the first place by the existence of the monastery and the possibility of rich pickings. Despite the fact that very little is known about St Donnan himself, no fewer than four monks of Eigg figure as saints in early Irish sources: Berchan, Enan, Congalach and Conan.

The monastery at Applecross was mentioned in Chapter 5 in the context of its Pictish connections. It was founded in AD 673 by an Irish monk from Bangor, Maelrubha. He had left Ireland two years previously, but it is not known where he spent those years – perhaps in Pictland, or perhaps at Iona. There is now no trace on the ground of his monastery, apart from a 3m-high (9ft 10in) cross-slab beside the gate into the modern churchyard and carved fragments inside the church, but the local Gaelic name a' Chomraich means protected place and reflects the sanctuary of the monastic precinct. Its location suggests that this would have been a large and wealthy monastery. Applecross Bay is a broad and sheltered landing-place, the valley is fertile and the river ran past the monastery (**58**).

Smaller monasteries

In the absence of historical records, it is often difficult to gauge the size and importance of ecclesiastical sites known from surface remains in the field. There has been very little excavation even of known monasteries, and the evidence hidden beneath the turf would undoubtedly transform our understanding of many sites. A good example of the complexity of even a small site is Ardwall Island, just off the Kirkcudbright coast in south-west Scotland. Excavations by Charles Thomas in the 1960s demonstrated that initially there was simply a small group of graves centred round a rock-cut hollow where a shrine may have stood. This was replaced by a

58 St Maelrubha chose Applecross Bay for his monastery.

small timber chapel with its contemporary graves, and finally the timber chapel was rebuilt in stone, the whole sequence spanning probably the sixth to eighth centuries. The site was not enclosed by an earthwork until the second or third phase of building, when its character became more formal. The burials here included those of men, women and children, which implies that this chapel served a lay population, despite its location on a small offshore island. A similar sequence could well be true of some of the small ecclesiastical sites in Argyll.

Adomnán refers to a dependent monastery founded from Iona in Tiree. He calls it Campus Luinge (the Plain of Luinge), which is not, unfortunately, helpful in trying now to identify it. Both the medieval parish churches of Tiree, at Kirkapoll and Soroby, were dedicated to St Columba. At Kirkapoll, an older chapel stands on a rocky outcrop, and two very simple linear crosses are carved on bare rock-faces, but they could be of any age. At Soroby, there is a simple slab incised with a ringed cross and, set in a boulder base, an ornate cross-slab which looks almost decadent in comparison with Iona's sculpture. Heavy cable mouldings and an over-large central roundel make this an extraordinary piece (59). More promising than either of these two sites is Ceann a' Mhara near the south-west tip of the island, from which point Iona is easily visible. Here a rocky knoll beside the shore has been enclosed with a sturdy wall; within are the remains of huts and a later medieval chapel. Three boulders bear sunken crosses.

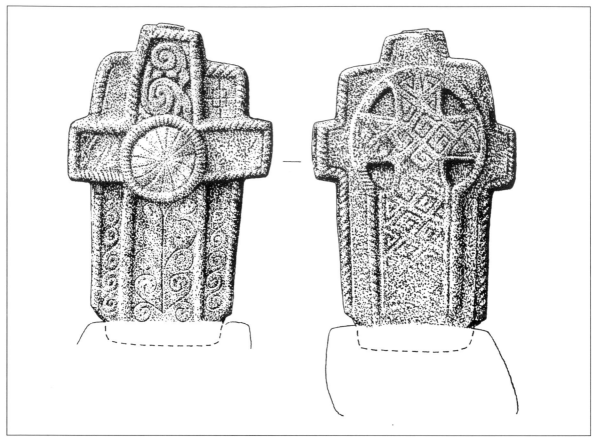

59 The cross-slab at Soroby, Tiree.

South of Skye are the islands of Canna, Rhum, Eigg and Muck. Three of these islands are known to have had ecclesiastical communities, a monastery in the case of Eigg and a hermitage in the case of Rhum (Becchan of Rhum died around 677), and Canna has a particular interest because it illustrates several aspects of the early church. At A' Chill above the island's major harbour, there was a medieval church dedicated to St Columba on a site of much greater antiquity, encapsulated in a sadly weathered but once splendid cross (60). This and other sculpture are thought to indicate the presence here of a monastery. In contrast to the domestic location of the supposed monastery, there are, on the south coast of the island, about 10km (6 miles) from A' Chill, substantial remains of a hermitage, built on a rocky ledge below very steep cliffs and thus very difficult to

reach either by land or water. The site is known as Sgòr nam Ban-naomha or Cliff of the Holy Women (**colour plate 10**), although this name is likely to relate to later use of the buildings. An oval area some 40m (131ft) across is enclosed within a stone wall 2m (6ft 6in) thick, and there are several small round or sub-rectangular buildings as well as a massive circular building. An unusual feature is the well-designed drainage system, with a stone-lined water-channel running across the enclosure, through a rectangular structure, perhaps a bath-house, built on to the inner face of the main wall and out through the wall.

South of Iona, in the Garvellach Isles, there may have been a small monastery on Eileach an Naoimh, but there may be a touch of wishful thinking about this site, which currently occupies an important place in the literature on

60 East face of the cross at A' Chill, Canna.

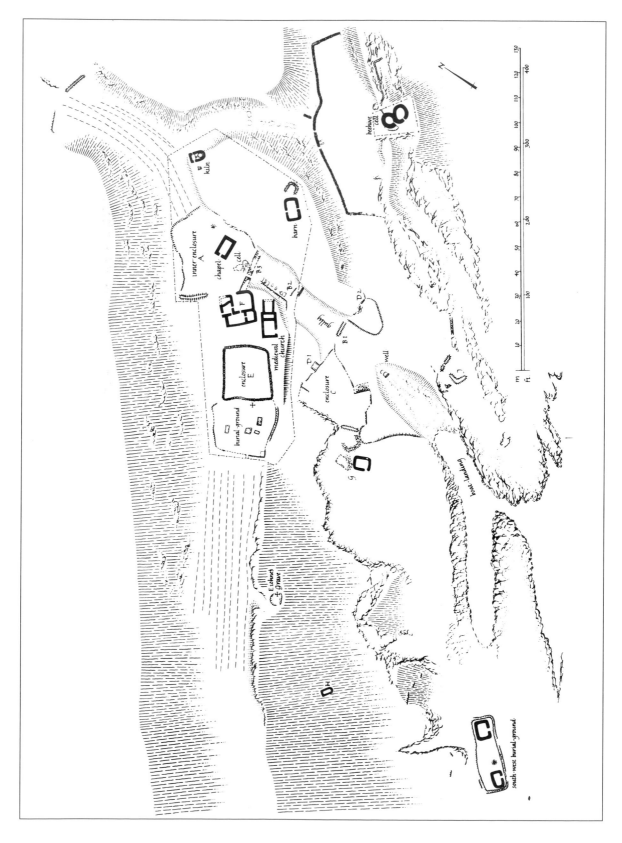

61 Plan of the early Christian and later remains on Eileach an Naoimh.

early Christianity in western Scotland. The wishful thinking began with the identification of the site as Adomnán's Hinba in the nineteenth century. There are, however, no early documentary references to the site, and its proposed function as an early monastery depends upon the remains of a stone-built 'beehive' cell and a possible grave. Its location is ideal for a small monastery and was certainly chosen for a medieval chapel of the eleventh or twelfth century. But the complex of structures and walls is complicated by later use of the site for farming purposes from the seventeenth century onwards (**61**). The 'beehive' cell is a double version of such cells known in Ireland; the western chamber is still partially roofed and has entrances both from the outside and from the other chamber (this structure is in state care;

62). Its age is undoubted, but 'beehive' cells are now recognized in Ireland as a feature more of secular than monastic settlements in the early Christian period. Eithne's Grave is as far west of the landing-place as the 'beehive' cell is to the east, both detached from the main complex. Eithne's Grave is a circular stony platform with a stone kerb and two upright slabs, one of which is incised with a cross. Local tradition no older than the nineteenth century associates this structure with Columba's mother, Eithne, but this again is wishful thinking, building on the supposition that this was the site of the Columban monastery of Hinba. In the absence of dating evidence, interpretation of this site must remain open, although the odds are probably on its monastic status. There are two more simple grave-markers with incised crosses from the island, but they are very difficult to date.

62 The stone 'beehive' cell on Eileach an Naoimh.

Another arrangement appears to have been the small offshore monastery serving a lay population on the mainland, the latter marked by a prayer-cross. This seems to have been the case on the Ardnave peninsula in northern Islay, where the Kilnave high cross may represent a centre of lay worship in the eighth century. The cross was carved in one piece from Torridonian flagstone, and it stands 2.63m (8ft 7in) high in a composite box-type base; it is a ringless cross, decorated only on its east face with predominantly spiral patterns. Excavations at nearby Kilellan have confirmed domestic activity in the area at least as late as the seventh century, when some unfortunate person lost a silver dress-pin set with red garnets. Just off the tip of the peninsula is Nave Island, where there are the remains of a medieval chapel within an enclosure which looks earlier and which has produced a fragment of a cross of probable eighth-century date.

A similar relationship may have existed between the community on Eilean Mór and that served by the high cross at Keills on the mainland some 6km (3.75 miles) to the north (p. 78), for both sites are associated with St Abban from Leinster. The tiny island of Eilean Mór in the Sound of Jura has an interesting ecclesiastical past. There is a well-preserved medieval chapel built in the early thirteenth century, with traces of its enclosure wall; this chapel is known to have had the patronage of the MacDonald Lords of the Isles in the fourteenth and fifteenth centuries. Close by is the shaft of a ringed cross which was probably set up in the tenth century (63). It is sadly damaged, but at least there are traces of the ring and enough of the decoration on the shaft to

63 The church and cross-shaft on Eilean Mór.

show that this was once a remarkable monument. There are panels and borders of interlace and key-pattern, along with a horse and hooded rider and somewhat ponderous yet ferocious animal ornament.

Near the south end of the island is a steep gully cutting into old sea-cliffs. Walling across the mouth of the gully forms a small building, perhaps an early chapel or house, from which there is access to a cave higher up in the gully (**64**). On the east wall of this small cave are carved a marigold cross and an encircled *chi–rho* cross on a short pedestal. If the high cross marked the site of a monastery, the cave may have been its hermitage.

Hermitages and caves

As well as those attached to nearby monasteries, there are many small hermitages on remote

64 The gully leading to the cave hermitage on Eilean Mór.

islands throughout the Hebrides as far as North Rona, which were the homes of monks looking for peace, meditation and an austere life in 'a desert place in the ocean'. Ian Fisher has suggested that the monks may also have seen themselves as 'guarding the frontier of Christendom against the demonic forces of the ocean'. There are a number of references to demons and other perils of the deep in Adomnán's *Life of Columba*.

The Rule of Colum Cille, enacted in the mid-eighth century, advised monks 'Be alone in a desert place apart in the neighbourhood of a chief monastery, if you distrust in your conscience to be in the company of many.' Such a desert place could be a lonely hut, but often it was a cave. St Martin of Tours had set an

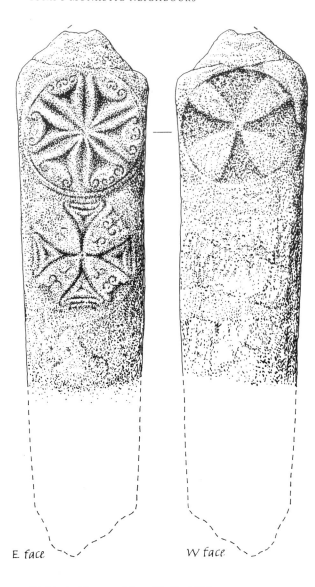

E face   W face

65 Marigold cross-slab at Cladh a' Bhile.

designated St Ciaran's Cave, and it contains not only a socket-stone for an upright cross but also a boulder carved with a fine marigold-type of cross within a T-fret border. Excavations in St Columba's Cave at Cove near Ellary on Loch Caolisport have demonstrated ecclesiastical use of the cave in the early Christian period as well as in later times.

On the west coast of Iona, there is a cave known as Uamh Mhartainn, St Martin's Cave. Although there is no evidence of ecclesiastical use for it, the coincidence between the name of the cave, the tradition of cave hermitages and the high cross of St Martin at the eighth-century monastery is very appealing. On the south coast of Mull, numerous small crosses carved on the walls of caves at Carsaig (Nuns' Cave) and Scoor indicate their use as retreats or refuges in early Christian and later medieval times.

Lay cemeteries

Sometimes it is difficult to fit a known but undocumented site into the monastic framework, and some such sites may be better viewed as lay cemeteries. A good example is the enchanting little cemetery hidden among the trees near Ellary, known as Cladh a' Bhile (Burial-ground of the Sacred Tree). The existing wall built in the late nineteenth century is thought to lie on the line of the original enclosure, and there are no traces of any chapel. Contained within the enclosure are almost thirty grave-markers, the largest collection in western Scotland outside Iona; most are modest in design, but a few are outstanding. The latter include a large pillar with an ornamented equal-armed cross below an equally beautiful marigold cross, probably dating to the eighth century (65). The cemetery would appear to have gone out of use after the eighth century. Any contemporary chapel would probably have been built in timber, and there is a noticeable gap in the distribution of the grave-markers on the west side of the enclosure, which could have held a small chapel orientated east–west.

example in the fourth century for retiring to a cave, and it was followed by many holy men. St Ninian's Cave at Physgill near the monastery of Whithorn in Galloway shows the classic relationship, as at Tours, of cave and monastery. Eilean Mór is an example on a lesser scale of a small monastery and cave hermitage, and there are many caves round the coast of Scotland which are dedicated to saints and which sometimes display incised crosses on their walls. A large cave on the coast of Kintyre is

8
Iona, Ireland and the Vikings

The great high crosses of Iona are the only physical traces on the island today of the enormous influence that the monastery commanded in the eighth century. By then, Iona was at the heart of a widespread and tightly knit family of monasteries and churches, which embraced Ireland, Dalriada and Pictland. At least two Irish kings retired to Iona in the second half of the eighth century – Niall Frossach, King of Tara, and Artgal, King of Connacht, while a third, Domnall, King of Tara, retired either to Iona or to Durrow. Columba was himself a highly influential man, and he forged strong links between his new monastery in Argyll and the Church in Ireland. Adomnán implies that there were at least five Columban monasteries in Ireland, but the names are known of only three of them: Durrow in County Offaly, Derry in County Down, and Drumhome in County Donegal. This network continued to expand, until a new political factor entered the scene – the Vikings. The life-threatening presence of Viking longships turned the Irish Sea into the Viking Sea, and the monastic dialogue between Ireland and Iona became, not impossible, but certainly at times very difficult. The west coast of Scotland, and the route north that John Marsden has called the 'sea-road of the saints', became increasingly dominated by Scandinavian raiders, traders and colonists as the ninth century passed.

Some of the events that punctuated this Scandinavian seepage were recorded by the writers of monastic annals. Iona's offspring on the Northumbrian coast, Lindisfarne, was sacked in 793, probably by Norwegian raiders based in Orkney. The following year, a terse entry in the *Annals of Ulster* records 'devastation of all the islands of Britain by the gentiles', and in 795 comes the first recorded attack on Iona, along with the island of Skye and monasteries in Ireland (**66**). Iona may have suffered again in 798, when it is recorded that there were raids throughout the Hebrides and Ulster, and it certainly was plundered and burned in 802, in 806 when sixty-eight monks were murdered, and again in 825. Raids on Irish monasteries appear to have been restricted to Ulster and Leinster until the third decade of the ninth century, when Viking activities spread farther south.

The annalists were inevitably most interested in recording raids on monasteries, and it can be assumed that secular homes of high status suffered as well. It is likely that earlier trading contacts had taught the Vikings that monasteries were the repositories of great wealth, to the extent that it was worth returning time and time again. Powerful lay patronage had ensured that there was worldly as well as spiritual treasure in the great churches, treasure of gold, silver and precious stones. Enough early church plate has survived to show its beauty and costliness, and there is a seventh-century description by Cogitosus of tombs 'adorned with a refined profusion of gold, silver, gems

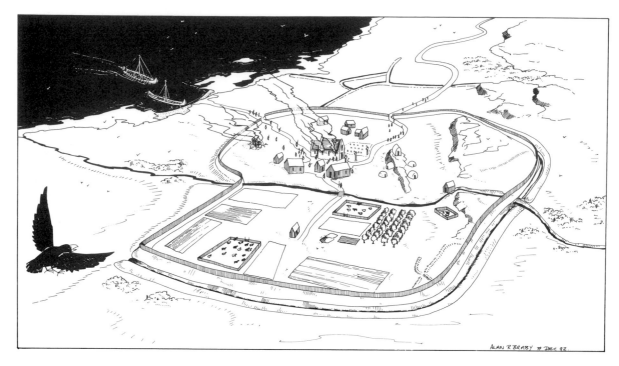

66 Artist's impression of the Columban monastery at the time of the first recorded Viking attack in 795.

and precious stones with gold and silver crowns hanging from above'. Monasteries also acted as places of safe-keeping for royal treasure.

The Vikings' knowledge of what they were seeking can be graphically illustrated by one of the raids on Iona. For once there is information beyond the brief entry in the annals, for a poem was written in honour of one of the slaughtered monks by Walafrid Strabo (died 849), the famed scholar and Abbot of Reichenau in southern Germany. The monk was Blathmac, who appears to have been acting as prior in the absence of Abbot Diarmait. Knowing that the raiders sought 'the precious metals wherein lie the holy bones of Columba', monks took the shrine and buried it. Blathmac sent away a number of the monks to hide. When the marauders arrived, 'threatening cruel perils to the blessed men', Blathmac and the monks who remained with him refused to reveal where the shrine was hidden and were duly killed.

There are several interesting aspects to this tale, aside from the fact that the Vikings appear

to have known about Columba's shrine or reliquary. The monks were forewarned of the raid, at least for long enough to hide the reliquary and to send some of the community to safety (presumably into the hilly interior of the island). This suggests that the monastery had a watchtower. Ann Hamlin has suggested that the tall stone towers of tenth-century Irish monasteries may have been preceded by wooden towers, as is implied in Bede's *Life of Cuthbert*. When St Cuthbert died on Farne Island in 687, the news was signalled to the monastery on Lindisfarne by lighting a beacon fire which was spotted from a watchtower on Lindisfarne. From such a tower on Iona, Viking ships could have been seen long before they entered the Sound of Iona (and it may have been from a watchtower that the monastery bell was rung even in earlier times). The fact that Blathmac and the Vikings understood one another on the subject of the whereabouts of the reliquary indicates the use of an interpreter, and Strabo's reference to 'the precious metals wherein lie the holy bones of Columba' confirms that by this time Columba's corporeal relics were housed in a casket or reliquary.

Hiding the casket by burying it was standard practice for safeguarding valuables in times of trouble until recent centuries. As the author of *Orkneyinga Saga* observed of later Norse raiders, 'The Hebrideans were so scared of them, they hid whatever they could carry either in among the rocks or underground.' The Norsemen themselves buried hoards of silver when the need arose. One hoard of Scandinavian type has been found on Iona, when a drainage trench was dug just north of the Abbey in 1950. It contained more than 350 silver coins, mostly Anglo-Saxon in origin, a small piece of gold rod, a silver ingot and an Anglo-Saxon ornamental mount, made of silver with gold filigree and a green glass setting (**67**). Both the mount and the coins suggest that the hoard was buried in the late tenth century, perhaps on the occasion of the raid recorded in 986, when the abbot and fifteen monks were killed. It is thought that the silver may have been brought to Iona by the Norse King of Dublin, Olaf Sihtricsson, who retired 'in penitence and pilgrimage' to the monastery in 980. Olaf had ruled at York before moving to Dublin. Among the coins were four struck at York during his time there. Another Viking silver hoard of similar date was found on the little island of Inchkenneth off the west coast of Mull.

The relics of St Columba

Just as Columba's bones were revered at Iona, Bishop Aidan's bones and those of St Cuthbert were revered at Lindisfarne. Thanks to Bede, more is known about the translation of Cuthbert's remains than of those of his colleagues. Cuthbert was first buried in 687 in a stone sarcophagus (a solid stone coffin) at the right of the altar in the Church of St Peter on Lindisfarne; eleven years later, the body was moved to a 'light chest' to be kept above ground in the same place. This 'enshrinement' of St Cuthbert is thought perhaps to have been the impetus for the making of the *Lindisfarne Gospels*. In Adomnán's time, the body of

67 Anglo-Saxon mount from the Viking Age hoard found on Iona.

Columba, wrapped in white linen, was still in its original grave, the precise location of which is not known; tradition places it beneath St Columba's Shrine. But there were already portable relics of St Columba in use at Iona, which are mentioned in Adomnán's *Life of Columba*.

These included garments (*vestimenta*), such as the white tunic (*candida tunica*) that he was wearing when he died, and books 'written with his own pen'. These relics were taken out of the church and used to avert disaster when necessary. For example, during a severe drought one spring, it was decided that some of the senior monks 'should go round the plain that had lately been ploughed and sown, taking with them the white tunic of Saint Columba, and books in his own handwriting; and should three times raise and shake in the air that tunic, which he wore in the hour of his departure from the flesh; and should open his books and read from them, on the hill of the angels' (II, 44).

But the principal relics of any saint were the bones. Columba's bones were clearly preserved in a metal reliquary by 825, when Blathmac and his fellow monks defended them with their lives; but it is not known whether these represented the complete skeleton or whether the bones had already been divided. The exact date of Columba's enshrinement is uncertain, but it must have taken place sometime between the death of Adomnán in 704 and the promulgation of the Rule of Colum Cille in Ireland in 753 (for which occasion the saint's relics would be required). Ian Fisher's argument is very persuasive, that the enshrinement and the creation of both the *Book of Kells* and the three early high crosses should be linked together and dated to the middle of the eighth century.

An exquisite reliquary exists today, known as the Monymusk reliquary (**68**), which was probably created in the eighth century, but it is tiny and could only have held a few small bones or fragments of bones. It consists of a wooden box covered with bronze and silver sheeting and decorative mounts, and it measures just 108mm long, 51mm wide and 98mm high (4.25 by 2.0 by 3.8in). The silver plates are incised with typically Pictish animals, and it is likely that the casket was made in Pictland. Tradition holds this to be the 'Brecbennoch of St Columba', one of the sacred battle ensigns of the Scottish army and used at the battle of Bannockburn in 1314. The Brecbennoch was associated with the lands

68 The Monymusk reliquary.

of Forglen in Banffshire, where the church is dedicated to St Adomnán, and after the battle it and the lands of Forglen passed into the care of Malcolm of Monymusk. If the Monymusk reliquary was created to hold bones of St Columba, it must have been after the bones had been divided between various churches, and that is another event of uncertain date.

The *Annals of Ulster* record that Abbot Diarmait of Kells and Iona took the reliquaries of St Columba to Scotland and returned with them to Ireland in 831. In 849, Kenneth mac Alpin, King of Scots and Picts, caused relics of St Columba to be transferred to a new church built for the purpose at Dunkeld, and the Abbot of Iona took relics to Ireland. Columba's crozier may have been taken to Dunkeld at the same time. St Columba's bones were thus formally divided between Scotland and Ireland, but some, presumably, stayed at Iona. In 878, the *Annals* record that the shrine of Columba and other relics came to Ireland to escape the Vikings; it is not made clear whence they came, but it was most probably from Iona.

George Henderson has suggested that these monastic treasures were welcomed 'officially' in Ireland and that the occasion was made the moment for the enshrining of the *Book of Durrow*, one of the treasures that came with the shrine, along with the *Book of Kells*.

Iona was not bereft of Columban relics for ever. At some stage a bone or bones of one of Columba's hands was returned to the island, for there is a record in the early fifteenth century of the gift to Iona by Donald, Lord of the Isles, of a gold and silver reliquary for the hand of St Columba. Books written by Columba also became holy relics, of which the most famous is the *Cathach*, a copy of the psalms enshrined within a silver-gilt box, which, like the Monymusk reliquary and St Columba's crozier, became a sacred battle ensign.

Iona in the ninth century

In contrast to Lindisfarne, where the monastery was finally abandoned after a raid in 875, Iona withstood the Viking onslaught and survived. Its resilience was based on a strategy of partial withdrawal, which seems to have been successful. In 804 land was acquired by Iona at Kells in County Meath, and the building there of a new monastery was underway by 807 and completed in 814, when, according to the *Annals of Ulster*, 'Cellach, abbot of Iona, having finished the construction of the church of Kells, resigned the headship, and Diarmait, foster-son of Daigre, was appointed in his place.' Thereafter, although abbots were still styled 'of Iona', they were as likely to be resident at Kells as at Iona. It is clear, from the records of Viking raids if nothing else, that a monastic presence at Iona was maintained long after the foundation of Kells.

Despite the horror expressed in these early records of Viking raids, they were not a novel experience for monastic communities, certainly in Ireland and to a lesser extent in Scotland. Irish annals record the burning of monasteries on no fewer than thirty occasions between 612 and 792, sometimes accidentally but sometimes caused by deliberate attacks by secular forces. In 793, for example, the year in which Lindisfarne was attacked by Vikings, the monastery of Armagh was ravaged and plundered by warriors of the Uí Chremthainn. There were also clerical wars, such as the battle in 764 between the monasteries of Clonmacnoise and Durrow in which 200 people of the Durrow community were killed. More understandable, perhaps, in the context of today were attacks caused by hardship. A great famine in 773 was followed by raids on monasteries; a devastating cattle plague in 777 was followed by attacks on the monasteries of Kildare, Clonmore and Kildalkey; and a very bad winter in 1095 caused a great loss of cattle, which was followed by attacks on at least nine monasteries. These attacks are all documented in Irish sources, but there are far fewer Scottish sources for the period. Irish monasteries were more closely tied to sources of secular power than most monasteries in Scotland; those in Dalriada with

69 The boat and Weland the Smith on a Viking Age cross-shaft.

vulnerable Irish allegiances were separated by the sea from easy attack, while Pictish monastic history is barely recorded.

But there is one hint that we should not be too complacent about the fortunes of monasteries in Scotland. This is the record of the burning of St Donnan's monastery in Eigg in 617. The identity of the attackers is not known, and some scholars have tried to argue that the tragedy should be seen as evidence of Viking raids long before the Viking Age proper opened in the last decade or so of the eighth century. But there is no supporting evidence for such an interpretation, and the Eigg episode is better understood, not necessarily alone, as part of 'the dangerous political games being played out around Ireland and Scotland in the early seventh century', in the words of Dáibhí Ó Cróinín.

To return to the ninth century, the history, let alone the archaeology, of Iona after the transfer of the leaders of the community to Kells is very difficult to evaluate in terms of number of inmates and extent of influence. But there is no doubt that a monastic community of some sort survived the next three centuries.

Viking age sculpture in Iona

Despite the presence of many pagan Viking graves on neighbouring islands such as Tiree, Colonsay, Oronsay and Islay, none has been

70 Graveslab incised with runes.

found on Iona. A pair of Scandinavian oval brooches were in the possession of a Mull landowner in the late nineteenth century but are now lost. Such brooches are often found in female Viking graves, but there is no guarantee that this pair was found in Mull. The Iona/Mull gap in the distribution of graves may be real and a reflection of the strength of native resistance to Norse settlement, particularly in the vicinity of the holy island of Iona. There are no Scandinavian place-names in Iona and only a handful of settlement-names in Mull.

By the later tenth century, many Norse families were becoming Christian. There appear to have been converted Norsemen among the community at Iona by this time, one of whom was the penitent king from Dublin already mentioned. Three gravestones carved to suit Norse taste have survived, all dating to the late tenth or early eleventh century. One is a fragment of the upper part of a narrow cross-slab (no. 94); it is made of a grey shaly sandstone best matched in the Isle of Man, and the style of decoration also suggests that it was imported, ready-made, from the Isle of Man. This was an upright grave-marker, as was a larger fragment (no. 95, **69**) decorated on one side with a panel of irregular plaitwork, beneath which is an animal with its tail knotted round its body. On the other side is part of a figural scene, with a boat carrying several warriors and a smith with a hammer in his hand and, in front of him, his punch, pincers and shears. This is surely Weland the Smith of Norse legend. The stone is black shale, probably from the island of Lismore. The third fragment is half of a recumbent graveslab carved with a double-ribbon cross with expanded terminals and a square interlaced round its centre (no. 69, **70**). Along its border runs a runic inscription, which reads 'Kali the son of Olvir laid this stone over his brother Fugl.'

9
Iona in medieval times

Neither history nor archaeology can shed much light on the fate of Iona in the three centuries after the foundation of Kells. A monastic community certainly survived on the island and was still held in high regard on both sides of the Irish Channel. At least one Pictish king and two Irish kings had been buried at Iona, and it was presumably the burial-place for kings of Dalriada. It was only after the royal dynasty had transferred itself eastwards into Pictland that the king-lists make a point of recording that Kenneth mac Alpin and his successors were buried at Iona. Indeed the phrase becomes quite monotonous: *et sepultus in Iona insula*, 'and was buried in the island of Iona', almost as if it were a scribal convention. The king-lists date from the twelfth century and later, and some doubt has been cast on how dependable they are as historical documents. Nevertheless, it seems very likely that Iona remained the primary burial-place for Scottish kings until the end of the eleventh century, after which that role passed to Dunfermline. The only surviving building of the monastery to which these royal burial-parties came is St Columba's Shrine.

St Columba's Shrine

Tucked in between the west end of the Abbey church and the west range of the cloister is a small building now known as St Columba's Shrine (**71, 72**). Originally, this chapel was free-standing, but its importance was evidently recognized by the builders of the Benedictine Abbey, and it was not only left in place but was soon incorporated into the Abbey complex. Much of the superstructure was rebuilt in 1962, but the original walls stood to a height of about 1m (3ft 3in) in the nineteenth century. The walls are about 0.5m (1ft 8in) thick, built of local flagstone (the modern restoration used quarried granite as well as flagstone), and the interior measures 3.2 by about 2.2m (10ft 6in by 7ft). The only direct dating evidence for this building is the fact that it existed before the adjacent angle-tower of the Abbey church was built in the fifteenth century. Luckily there are two other good clues to an early date. The original masonry of the side-walls projects at the west end (**73**). This is a feature of early Irish churches, where the projecting walls are known as *antae* and extend the full height of the building; *antae* are believed to originate in the design of earlier timber churches. The fact that here the doorway and the *antae* were faced with dressed stone suggests that St Columba's Shrine is not earlier than the ninth or tenth century, although it may well have had a timber predecessor. The second clue to its age is historical. According to the Icelandic saga *Heimskringla*, the Norwegian king Magnus Barelegs visited the 'small church of Columcille' at Iona in 1098, then still intact, even to its wooden door.

The site of this chapel, with its traditional association with St Columba, may mark the saint's original burial-place, venerated long after

71 The restored Abbey in 1974. In the foreground are the medieval paved street and bakehouse.

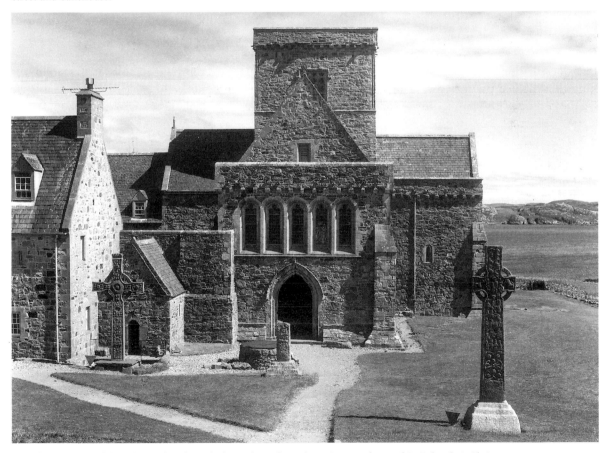

72 The west end of the Abbey church, with the replica of St John's Cross in front of St Columba's Shrine, the shaft of St Matthew's Cross (now in the Abbey museum) near the well and St Martin's Cross.

73 The front of St Columba's Shrine with its projecting *antae*, and graveslabs reused as paving.

his bones had been lifted and used as relics. St John's Cross stood just 5m (16ft) to the west, and the main church of the monastery is thought to have been on the site of the later Abbey church to the south-east. Two stone coffins still lie beneath the modern wooden floor, but these are probably of late medieval date. The area in front of the chapel was paved in later times with reused graveslabs.

It is not known where the various kings were buried, nor can any of the surviving sculpture be related to them. It is difficult in any case to know what to expect in the way of early royal tombstones. In Pictland, both Meigle and St Vigeans had royal connections and were burial-places of the ninth and tenth centuries. Their surviving sculpture suggests that wealthy patrons commissioned elaborately decorated

slabs to lie on top of their graves. At Govan in British Strathclyde, someone important in the ninth century was buried in a carved stone sarcophagus, presumably kept above ground in the church. But at Iona, as we have seen, ostentatious grave furniture seems to have been eschewed, certainly by the monks, and perhaps even by kings.

St Oran's Chapel and Reilig Odhráin

Reilig Odhráin, the burial-ground around St Oran's Chapel, is likely to have been in use, perhaps for important laymen, at this time. In its present form, the visible enclosure dates only to 1875, but the site had been in use as a burial-ground for centuries, and the discovery there of many of the extant early Christian grave-markers suggests that its use goes back into the eighth century at least. St Oran's Chapel itself was added in the twelfth century, probably built as a family burial chapel by Somerled, 'king' of the Isles, who died in 1164, or by his son Reginald. The later Lords of the Isles continued to be buried there, even after a chapel had been built at the meeting-place of the Council of the Isles at Finlaggan in Islay.

St Oran's Chapel (**74**) is the earliest intact building to survive of the early monastery, and the first obvious trace of the Abbey complex that the visitor encounters following the modern road from the village past the St Columba Hotel. It is a very attractive building with its decorative arched doorway and modern slate roof (restoration took place in 1957). The type of building and the decorated arch are similar to those of Irish churches of the later twelfth century, and they show that new building was still being carried out in the Irish idiom at Iona at that date. At some stage in later medieval times, masonry was removed from the left-hand wall beside the doorway, presumably to hold a lamp or a holy-water stoup. Inside, the simple rectangular chapel is lit from two windows and floored with slabs, including seven medieval graveslabs. Another graveslab is raised on a stone setting against the south wall, close to a splendidly carved tomb-recess (**75**). Its design suggests that this recess was built late in the fifteenth century, but the identity of its occupant is uncertain beyond the likelihood that he was a Lord of the Isles. The reconstructed altar at the east end stands on an early foundation. The

75 The fifteenth-century tomb-recess in St Oran's Chapel.

traditional dedication of both chapel and burial-ground is to St Oran (Odhráin), cousin to Columba.

Many of the later medieval graveslabs found in Reilig Odhráin are now in the Abbey museum, but a few weathered examples can still be seen in the burial-ground. They were all lying jumbled together until about 1859, when the Duke of Argyll caused them to be set in two parallel rows and enclosed within iron railings. The two rows were known as 'the ridge of the kings' and 'the ridge of the chiefs' (**76**). There are about one hundred and fifty medieval graveslabs, together with eleven effigies and ten complete or fragmentary crosses. Many of these carvings are the work of a distinctive Iona school of sculpture. The effigies represent five warriors, five abbots and a prior.

From the north side of Reilig Odhráin, a cobbled 'street' runs past St Martin's Cross; formerly this connected the Abbey with St Oran's Chapel and continued southwards across Reilig Odhráin. It was revealed by excavation in 1962 and appears to date originally from the time of the construction of the Abbey. As visible today, it runs towards St Martin's Cross and then along the stone revetment to the medieval bakehouse, but it is assumed that formerly it forked and the eastern branch ran to the Abbey. (The revetment was built around 1840 to replace an earlier

74 St Oran's Chapel with its carved doorway.

76 St Oran's Chapel and Reilig Odhráin in 1965.

77 Sketch of Cladh an Dìsirt by J. Drummond about 1866.

Cladh an Diesart - Iona

enclosure wall.) This street, now known as the Street of the Dead, is part of a system of early tracks linking the Abbey to the Nunnery, to St Ronan's Bay and to Martyrs' Bay.

Cladh an Dìsirt

In 1164, the same year in which Somerled died, an Irish monk entered in his annals the last detailed record of the Columban monastery at Iona. One of its leading members was designated as *disertach*, head of the hermitage. Exactly where the hermitage was situated is unknown, but traces of its burial-ground can still be seen north-east of the Abbey. Known as Cladh an Dìsirt, Burial-place of the Hermitage, the site is not easy to understand from the surviving scant remains, but there appears to have been a small rectangular chapel within a walled enclosure. A drawing made in the mid-nineteenth century shows the walling of the enclosure to have been very delapidated on either side of an entrance formed by two large upright stones with a stone lintel (77). The two uprights are still visible today. A modern track leads south-eastwards to Port an Dìsirt, perhaps on the line of an earlier track giving access to the sea.

There are no other structures extant that can be dated prior to the Abbey complex, but the sanctity of the Irish monastery continued through the second half of the twelfth century. Godred, King of Man, was buried at Iona in 1187. Until 1156, Mull and Islay were part of the kingdom of Man, but thereafter they were controlled by Somerled and later his son, whose patronage was enjoyed by the monastery at Iona. But by the end of the century, the future of the Irish monastic community was in jeopardy. It was probably Somerled's son, Reginald, who made the decision to break with the past and to found a Benedictine house at Iona, and his new foundation met with predictable opposition from the Columban family of monasteries in Ireland. The chief monastery by now was Derry, and the *Annals of Ulster* for 1204 record that 'a monastery was made by Cellach, in the middle of the enclosure of Iona, in violation of the rights of the community of Iona'. Such was the fury in Ireland that a body of clergy, led by the Bishops of Tyrone and Tirconnell and the Abbots of Armagh and Derry, sailed to Iona with the intention of destroying the intruding monastery. Whatever the immediate outcome, this opposition had no lasting effect.

The endowment of the Benedictine monastery included lands in Iona, Mull, Islay, Coll, Colonsay, Oronsay and in Lorn, some of which are likely to have belonged to the Columban monastery. Reginald also founded the only Cistercian abbey in the western Highlands at Saddell in Kintyre.

Benedictine monks

Benedictine monasticism takes its name from St Benedict of Nursia, who drew up rules for the guidance of his community of monks at Monte Cassino in southern Italy sometime around AD 525. These rules for a life of poverty, chastity and obedience were gradually adopted elsewhere. Over the centuries, the original ideals became diluted, and from the tenth to the thirteenth century there were various attempts to reform monasticism by founding stricter orders, such as the Cluniac and Cistercian monks. It is thought that the first Benedictine community in Scotland was founded by St Margaret at Dunfermline soon after 1070. Apart from the Abbey at Iona, there were also Benedictine priories at Coldingham in Berwickshire, on the Isle of May off the coast of Fife, at Rhynd in Perthshire and at Urquhart in Moray. Iona was the latest of these foundations in Scotland, but several Benedictine houses were founded at the same period in Ireland. Benedictine monks were also known as the Black Monks, because they wore black habits.

The Benedictine Abbey at Iona

Iona Abbey is often known as St Mary's Abbey, but this was by tradition the dedication of the Abbey church rather than the monastery as a whole, which retained the dedication to

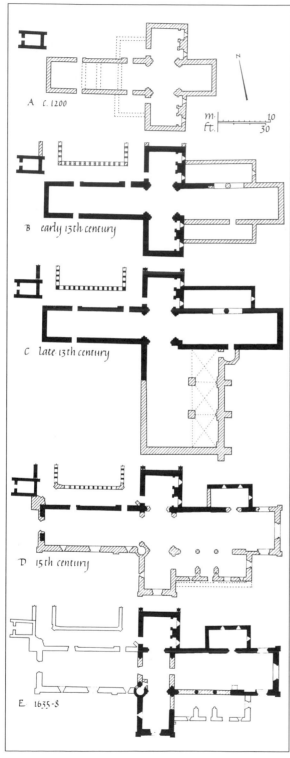

A c.1200

B early 13th century

C late 13th century

D 15th century

E 1635-8

78 Plans showing how the design of the church was modified over the centuries between about 1200 and the 1630s.

St Columba (see **colour plate 5**). This was a fine medieval abbey, much of which survived to be restored in the late nineteenth and the twentieth century, in stark contrast to its more famous Columban predecessor, of which so little remains. The church was built in Romanesque style during the first two decades of the thirteenth century, probably by Irish stonemasons. It was a cruciform building with a nave, transepts and chancel. The nave was the least well-preserved part of the church prior to the modern restoration, but, even so, there are hints in the surviving medieval masonry that it may have incorporated part of the nave of an earlier twelfth-century church. This has important implications for the vitality of the pre-Benedictine monastic community. Short nave-aisles were added to provide access between the nave and the transepts without using the crossing (shown by broken line on the plan (**78**, **A**)). Only the north transept survives, with a pair of round-arched chapels built within the thickness of its east wall (**79**). The church was modified even before it was finished by extending the chancel to the east, to form an aisled choir above a crypt (see **78**, **B**; **80**). This was a reflection perhaps of the expanding community, for whom domestic quarters were built to the north of the church in the course of the thirteenth century. The hallmarks of this early thirteenth-century work are pointed arches and dog-tooth ornament. Late in that century, the foundations of an enlarged south transept were laid out but apparently never finished (see **78**, **C**). Nothing more was done to the church until the mid-fifteenth century, when the east wall of the choir and the entire south wall of the church were demolished. The rebuilding provided a wider nave and choir, and a south aisle to the choir (see **78**, **D**). The building was embellished with fine traceried windows and rich carving.

The massive central tower was also built at this time. Above the belfry in the tower, there was an ingenious solution to both practical and spiritual needs in the form of a dovecote; this

79 Inside the north transept of the thirteenth-century Abbey church, two small chapels were built into the thickness of the wall.

provided variety in the diet of the community, as well as a neat symbol of Colum Cille himself, the Dove of the Church.

Most of the restored church of today is essentially of fifteenth-century build, apart from the north transept and the sacristy of the thirteenth century. The 'Michael Chapel', a detached chapel to the north of the Abbey church, is thought to have been built around 1200, perhaps for the use of the monks while the main church was being built (81). The cloister and main core of monastic buildings were added on the north side of the church. This

is relatively unusual, for in most monasteries the cloister ranges were built to the south of the church, in order that the latter, the tallest building, should not block out the light and warmth from the cloister. But at Iona, the location of the church was probably dictated by the desire to build on the same spot as the earlier church of the Columban monastery, and the location of the cloister by the need for

80 The restored choir of the church and the presbytery beyond.

81 The east side of the Abbey with the detached 'Michael Chapel' and the infirmary (now the Abbey museum).

82 Aerial view of the Abbey, identifying the major elements mentioned in the text.

running water. Water was essential for the domestic life of the community, and the nearest source was the Mill Stream to the north. The oldest parts of the claustral buildings are the windows in the east range and the chapter-house arcade. The north range belongs to the late thirteenth century, including the refectory where the monks ate their meals, and the reredorter or latrine, linked to the dormitory in

the east range (82). The reredorter is also linked to the Abbot's House, now a wholly restored building. The Rule of St Benedict required the whole monastic community to live together, including the abbot, but, as monasteries grew in size and complexity, this ideal became unrealistic. But the spirit of the ideal could be maintained by a physical link between the Abbot's House and the living quarters of the monks. The chapter-house was rebuilt in the late fifteenth century, protruding outwards from the east range of the cloister. This was where the

83 Fifteenth-century carving and inscription on one of the capitals of the crossing in the church.

monks gathered each day to listen to a chapter from the Rule of St Benedict. The detached building to the east of the refectory range is thought to have been the infirmary, built in the early thirteenth century; it has been entirely rebuilt as part of the modern restoration, and it now serves as a museum (see 81).

The west range of claustral buildings is entirely modern, although earlier foundations are known to have existed. The original range is likely to have included the kitchen. The foundations of a separate medieval bakehouse can still be seen to the immediate west of the Abbey (see 71).

The structural history of the Abbey over the centuries, including the restoration works in the late nineteenth and twentieth centuries, is fascinating but complex, and it is fully recorded in the *Iona* volume of the Royal Commission on the Ancient and Historical Monuments of Scotland. There is much of interest and beauty about both old and new, from the inscription recording the name of a master-mason of the fifteenth century carved on a capital in the crossing of the church (83) to the superb foliage and birds carved in modern times on the new columns of the cloister arcades (84). Both the Abbey and the Nunnery are set into their wider Scottish context in Richard Fawcett's book on *Scottish Abbeys and Priories*.

The village of Iona in the early thirteenth century must have been crowded and busy, with imported stonemasons and workmen, and cargoes of red granite from the Ross of Mull

and yellow sandstone from Carsaig on the south coast of Mull. For it was not just the Abbey that was under construction, but also the Nunnery.

The Nunnery and St Ronan's Chapel

The Nunnery was founded around 1200, like the Abbey probably by Reginald, but this time with a vested family interest in the sense that his sister, Bethoc, was the first prioress of this house of Augustinian canonesses. This was one of only two houses for this order in Scotland (the other was at Perth), although they were common in Ireland. The term Augustinian relates to St Augustine of Hippo (died AD 430), whose teaching the monks followed. The purpose of Augustinian canons was in part to serve the needs of the lay population, and it is particularly interesting to find that the Nunnery at Iona appears to have been established on the same spot as an earlier chapel and lay cemetery (see p. 46).

The Nunnery with its church and cloister is effectively a smaller version of the Abbey, and it is in fact one of the best-preserved medieval nunneries in the British Isles (85). The design of the church remains as it was built in the early thirteenth century, and it offers a good impression of the appearance of the original Abbey church. The attached east range of domestic buildings, including the chapter-house, is also original thirteenth-century work. The cloister was enlarged in the fifteenth century, with the refectory in the south range.

The church was designed with a rectangular nave and chancel, an aisle along the north side

84 Old and new columns in the Abbey cloister.

85 The Nunnery with the Ross of Mull in the distance.

of the nave, and a small chapel at the east end of the aisle (**86, 87**). Both the chancel and the aisle-chapel had vaulted ceilings, but only the chapel is now intact (**88**). Otherwise, the best-preserved parts of the church are the west gable and north wall of the nave, with narrow windows linked by a prominent string-course above the rounded arches that led into the aisle. With its warm stonework and modern flower-beds in the cloister, the Nunnery is a very pleasant place to linger on a sunny day. Enough carved fragments survive to show how attractive the cloister was

in the fifteenth century (**89**). The fragments are preserved in the Abbey museum, and there are numerous graveslabs from the Nunnery in both the Abbey museum and in St Ronan's Chapel. One of the most striking sixteenth-century graveslabs in the Abbey museum is a legacy from the Nunnery. It commemorates Prioress Anna MacLean, who died in 1543, and the surviving fragment depicts Prioress Anna herself with a pair of lap-dogs at her waist (no. 204). This is one of the latest medieval carvings at Iona.

To the north of the Nunnery, St Ronan's Chapel has been restored as a sculpture museum

86 The interior of the thirteenth-century Nunnery church, showing the rounded arches of the nave-arcade.

87 A small chapel projects from the north wall of the church.

88 The ribbed vault of the north chapel, the only intact part of the church.

(90). It was built around 1200 as the parish church for the island, and it is a simple rectangular building. The doorway and the west gable are entirely modern, but the other walls are largely original, although the north and south windows have been restored. Below the east window, the modern altar was built on the original medieval foundations. Excavations have revealed that this church was built on the site of an earlier chapel (see p. 46).

St Mary's Chapel

In a field south of the Abbey are the fragmentary remains of a chapel dedicated to St Mary, which was built probably in the thirteenth century. The fact that it lies close to the medieval track leading from St Ronan's Chapel to the Abbey suggests that it was intended in part for the use of pilgrims, for the cult of St Columba was popular at least until the sixteenth century.

89 Artist's impression of the fifteenth-century cloister-arcade in the Nunnery.

90 St Ronan's Chapel in 1973 before restoration.

The medieval streets

This track is shown on an estate map of 1769, where it is labelled 'Street'. The stretch between St Ronan's and MacLean's Cross lies beneath the modern road; at the cross, the modern road diverges north-westwards, whereas the medieval street kept the same alignment northwards, before swinging a little to the east past St Mary's. In 1764, this main street was described as being about 15 feet wide (4.6m) and built of large slabs of red granite. In 1769, there were five cottages along the east side of the street beyond the cross, and others scattered between the Nunnery and the sea. MacLean's Cross marks the point at which two other medieval tracks joined the street. One skirted Cnoc Mór on the west side of the Nunnery and ran originally to Martyrs' Bay, and this was known as Sràid nam Marbh or Street of the Dead. The other ran south-east to St Ronan's Bay. The

main village street of today, facing St Ronan's Bay, was created around 1800 (see **colour plate 4**). In earlier times the lay population is likely to have been more scattered, except during major periods of building works on the Abbey and the Nunnery. At those times, when the population was swelled with masons and other artisans, a village must have sprung up. Local tradition holds that there was once a village above Maol farm, on the south side of Cnoc Mór; this could explain the route taken by the medieval track from Martyrs' Bay to the Abbey. Medieval burials have been found at the head of the bay, and an old burial-ground, no longer visible, existed a little to the south-west. Its name was Cladh nan Druineach, which gave rise to the idea that it was somehow connected with the druids. The word *druineach* is now thought to mean craftsmen, and it is possible that this

91 The late medieval MacLean's Cross with its intricate interlaced decoration.

burial-ground was associated with stonemasons working on the Abbey and the Nunnery.

MacLean's Cross

At the junction of the three medieval streets and now beside the modern road between the Nunnery and the Abbey stands a striking example of the Iona school of late medieval carving, MacLean's Cross (no. 212). It is thought to date from the late fifteenth century and to have been commissioned as a wayside prayer-cross by the Clan MacLean (**colour plate 12**). There was once an inscription on a panel with a carving of a mounted warrior at the foot of the cross, but unfortunately the letters are no longer legible. The cross is carved from a single thin slab of chlorite-schist, and it stands fully 3.15m (10ft 4in) high above its base (**91**). Most of the decoration consists of interlaced plaitwork and foliage, but a pair of animals is visible at the top of the shaft on the east face, and the central disc on the front face of the cross-head has a depiction of Christ on the Cross.

The end of monastic life on Iona

Monastic life was flourishing on Iona in the fifteenth century, with wealth and patronage to fund extensive refurbishment both of the Abbey and of the Nunnery. But the new buildings were not to be in use for long. The Scottish Reformation of 1560 put an end to monastic life in Iona as elsewhere, and both the Abbey and the Nunnery began to fall into disrepair. There was an attempt in the 1630s to restore the eastern end of the Abbey church for use as the cathedral of the diocese of the Isles and later as the parish church. The ruined house on the north side of the Mill Stream belongs to this period. Tigh an Easbuig, the Bishop's House, is thought to have belonged to Bishop Neil

Campbell, and it is a rare example of unfortified domestic building of the early seventeenth century. But this reuse of the Abbey was short-lived, and from the 1660s until 1829 Iona lacked even its own minister. The Abbey and the Nunnery gradually disintegrated into the romantic ruins beloved of eighteenth-century visitors to the Scottish islands.

Interest in Iona blossomed in the nineteenth century, until in 1874–6 major repairs both to the Abbey and the Nunnery were carried out by the renowned architect Rowand Anderson. In 1899 the Duke of Argyll transferred ownership of the Abbey, the Nunnery and St Oran's Chapel to the Iona Cathedral Trust, with the condition that the Trust would restore the Abbey church and make it fit again for worship. This restoration was completed in 1910. With the foundation of the Iona Community by George MacLeod in 1938, work began on restoring the range of monastic buildings to designs prepared by the eminent conservation architect Ian G. Lindsay. The entire island of Iona was sold to the Fraser Foundation in 1979 (apart from the Abbey and Nunnery, and St Oran's Chapel, which already belonged to the Iona Cathedral Trust). The Fraser Foundation presented the island to the Scottish nation in memory of Lord Fraser of Allander, and the Secretary of State for Scotland transferred ownership to the National Trust for Scotland. The future of this sacred island and its historic monuments is thus secure, but far from static, for work on the Abbey and the Nunnery has continued, and plans for a visitor centre at Fionnphort on the Ross of Mull confirm that Iona and its buildings and sculpture will survive. Pilgrims of the twenty-first century will be able to explore the remains of the monastery first created by St Columba in the sixth century.

Places to visit

Most sites in Iona are described in greater detail in the text and are listed here, with their National Grid References, from the village northwards, westwards and southwards. Guided tours are arranged in the summer months along 'The Pilgrimage Route', which takes in several of the main sites. A visitor centre is planned for Fionnphort on the Ross of Mull, where the story of Iona will be explored.

Nunnery (NM 284240)
Founded around 1200 as a priory of Augustinian canonesses. Parts of the church and of the east and south ranges of domestic buildings survive round the cloister (see pp. 108–13).

St Ronan's Chapel and museum (NM 285241)
Built around 1200 as the parish church for the island. Restored and used as a sculpture museum (see pp. 46, 113).

MacLean's Cross (NM 285242)
Erected probably in the late fifteenth century by the Clan MacLean as a prayer-cross; richly carved (see pp. 114–16).

Parish church and manse (NM 285242)
Built in 1828, the church and manse were part of a series built in the Highlands of Scotland in response to an Act of Parliament and supervised by Thomas Telford. The manse is now an excellent heritage centre in which the story of Iona is presented.

Blàr Buidh (NM 284243)
A small prehistoric kerb-cairn, probably covering a burial (see p. 25).

St Oran's Chapel and Reilig Odhráin (NM 286244)
A twelfth-century chapel with a fine fifteenth-century tomb-recess, set in a burial-ground which has been in use since early Christian times and is still in use today (see pp. 100–2).

Abbey and museum (NM 2824)
Remains of the Columban monastery include the vallum (pp. 36–40), Tòrr an Aba (p. 41), the high crosses (pp. 67–76) and St Columba's Shrine (pp. 98–100). The Benedictine Abbey was founded around 1200. The restored buildings include the church, the cloister and associated domestic buildings, the 'Michael Chapel' and the infirmary (now a sculpture museum) (see pp. 103–8).

St Mary's Chapel (NM 287244)
The remains of a chapel built probably in the thirteenth century (see pp. 113–14).

Tigh an Easbuig (NM 287245)
'The Bishop's House' of the early seventeenth century was a simple rectangular building with two rooms on the ground floor. Best preserved

today is the partition wall between the two rooms. The larger room was a hall rising to the gabled roof, while the smaller room was the kitchen with a bedchamber on an upper floor (see p. 116).

Cladh an Dìsirt (NM 289248)
Remains of a burial-ground and chapel of the twelfth century (see p. 103).

Port na Frainge (NM 290252)
An immense granite boulder left by the Ice Age and recent boat-nausts (see pp. 17, 19).

Cobhan Cùilteach (NM 276249)
The remains of a circular stone hut and nearby enclosure (see p. 45).

Dùn Bhuirg (NM 264247)
A prehistoric fort perched on a rocky hill on the west coast of the island (see pp. 27–8).

St Columba's Bay
At the south end of the island, this is traditionally St Columba's first landing-place on Iona. Separated by a rocky ridge are Port na Curaich (NM 263217), with the long mound popularly thought to cover the saint's currach, and Port an Fhir-bhréige (NM 262219), with its strange pebble-built cairns (see pp. 25–6, 34).

Làraichean (NM 261218)
Remains of post-medieval stock-enclosures and buildings (see p. 19).

Marble quarry (NM 268217)
Dramatic quarry with industrial machinery and buildings (see pp. 17–18).

Port na Mairtir (NM 284238)
The traditional landing-place for coffins and a mound on which the coffins were rested (see p. 18).

Further reading

General and recent history

Beith, Mary *Healing Threads: Traditional Medicines of the Highlands and Islands*, Edinburgh University Press, Edinburgh, 1995.

Chapman, R.W. (ed.) *Johnson's Journey to the Western Islands of Scotland and Boswell's Journal of a Tour to the Hebrides with Samuel Johnson, LL.D.*, Oxford University Press, London, 1924.

Dunbar, John G. and Fisher, I. *Iona: A Guide to the Monuments*, HMSO, Edinburgh, 1995.

Duncan, A.A.M. *Scotland: The Making of the Kingdom*, Mercat Press, Edinburgh, 1989.

Iona Community *Iona: A Map*, Bartholomew, Edinburgh, 1983.

Lynch, Michael *Scotland: A New History*, Pimlico, London, 1992.

MacArthur, E. Mairi *Iona: The Living Memory of a Crofting Community 1750–1914*, Edinburgh University Press, Edinburgh, 1990.

MacArthur, E. Mairi (ed.) *That Illustrious Island ... Iona through Travellers' Eyes*, The New Iona Press, Iona, 1991.

MacArthur, E. Mairi *Columba's Island: Iona from Past to Present*, Edinburgh University Press, Edinburgh, 1995.

Ritchie, A. and Ritchie, E. *Iona Past and Present, with Maps*, Highland Home Industries, Edinburgh, 1928.

Ritchie, Graham and Harman, Mary *Argyll and the Western Isles*, HMSO, Edinburgh, 1995.

Ritchie, Graham and Ritchie, Anna *Scotland: Archaeology and Early History*, Edinburgh University Press, Edinburgh, 1991.

Royal Commission on the Ancient and Historical Monuments of Scotland *Argyll: An Inventory of the Monuments,* vol. 3, *Mull, Tiree, Coll and Northern Argyll*; vol. 4, *Iona*, HMSO, Edinburgh, 1980 and 1982.

Viner, David *The Iona Marble Quarry*, The New Iona Press, Iona, 1992.

Prehistory

Johnstone, Paul *The Sea-craft of Prehistory*, Routledge & Kegan Paul, London and Henley, 1980.

Ritchie, Graham (ed.) *The Prehistory of Argyll*, Edinburgh University Press, Edinburgh, 1997.

Wickham-Jones, Caroline *Scotland's First Settlers*, Batsford, London, 1994.

Early historic times

Anderson, A.O. and Anderson, M.O. (eds) *Adomnan's Life of Columba*, Nelson, Edinburgh, 1961; second edition, Oxford University Press, Oxford, 1991.

Anderson, M.O. *Kings and Kingship in Early Scotland*, Scottish Academic Press, Edinburgh, 1973.

Barber, J. 'Excavations on Iona, 1979', *Proceedings of the Society of Antiquaries of Scotland*, 111 (1981), 282–380.

Bede *A History of the English Church and People*, trs. L. Sherley-Price, Penguin Books, London, 1955.

Clancy, Thomas Owen and Márkus, Gilbert

Iona: The Earliest Poetry of a Celtic Monastery, Edinburgh University Press, Edinburgh, 1995.

Crawford, Barbara E. *Scandinavian Scotland*, Leicester University Press, Leicester, 1987.

Driscoll, S.T. and Nieke, M.R. *Power and Politics in Early Medieval Britain and Ireland*, Edinburgh University Press, Edinburgh, 1988.

Fawcett, Richard *Scottish Abbeys and Priories*, Batsford, London, 1994.

Fisher, Ian 'The monastery of Iona in the eighth century', in O'Mahony, Felicity (ed.) *The Book of Kells*, Scolar Press, Aldershot, 1994.

Foster, Sally *Picts, Gaels and Scots*, Batsford, London, 1995.

Henderson, George *From Durrow to Kells: The Insular Gospel-books 650–800*, Thames and Hudson, London, 1987.

Herbert, M. *Iona, Kells and Derry: The History and Hagiography of the Monastic Familia of Columba*, Oxford University Press, Oxford, 1988.

Hughes, K. and Hamlin, A. *The Modern Traveller to the Early Irish Church*, SPCK, London, 1977.

McCormick, Finbar 'Excavations at Iona, 1988', *Ulster Journal of Archaeology*, 56 (1993), 78–108.

Marsden, John *Sea-Road of the Saints: Celtic Holy Men in the Hebrides*, Floris Books, Edinburgh, 1995.

Nicholl, Eric H. (ed.) *A Pictish Panorama: The Story of the Picts and a Pictish Bibliography*, The Pinkfoot Press, Balgavies, Angus, 1995.

Ó Cróinín, Dáibhí *Early Medieval Ireland 400–1200*, Longman, London and New York, 1995.

O'Sullivan, Jerry 'Excavation of an early church and a women's cemetery at St Ronan's medieval parish church, Iona', *Proceedings of the Society of Antiquaries of Scotland*, 124 (1994), 327–65.

Ritchie, Anna *Picts*, HMSO, Edinburgh, 1989.

Ritchie, Anna *Viking Scotland*, Batsford, London, 1993.

Sharpe, Richard *Adomnán of Iona: Life of St Columba*, Penguin Books, London, 1995.

Smyth, Alfred P. *Warlords and Holy Men: Scotland AD 80–1000*, Edward Arnold, London, 1984.

Thomas, Charles *Celtic Britain*, Thames and Hudson, London, 1986.

Glossary

anta A buttress-like extension of the side-walls of a building.

broch A stone-built fortified dwelling with high walls, unique to Scotland.

cairn A mound of stones.

chancel The east end of a simple church, containing the altar.

choir The east end of a developed church, reserved for the use of the monks or clergy.

cist A pit lined and covered with stone slabs to act as a coffin.

crannog An artificial, or partly artificial, island on which dwellings have been built.

crossing In a cruciform church, the junction of the nave, transepts and choir.

cross-slab A slab of stone carved with a cross and set upright (as opposed to a free-standing cross).

cup-mark A small hollow carved into stone.

currach A boat with a wooden frame covered in hide.

drystone Built with stones but without mortar.

dun A small stone-built fortified farmstead.

geophysical survey Non-intrusive plotting of subterranean features by scientific methods.

high cross A tall free-standing stone cross.

Ice Age Period of glacial conditions, when ice covered the land.

kelp Seaweed, and the alkaline ash produced by burning seaweed.

kerb-cairn A mound of stones with a kerb of large boulders, covering a burial.

lintel A horizontal stone slab spanning an opening in a wall.

logboat A boat made in one piece by hollowing out a tree-trunk.

machair Low-lying flat land formed of shell-sand, usually supporting good pasture.

Mesolithic The period after the end of the Ice Age, when Scotland was settled by people who lived by hunting, fishing and gathering wild plants.

Neolithic A life-style based on mixed farming and the use of stone tools; it gradually succeeded the Mesolithic, and was replaced, after the introduction of metalworking, by the Bronze Age.

penannular brooch A circular metal hoop with a gap allowing the pin to pass through the hoop to fasten it to clothing.

presbytery The part of a church, east of the choir, reserved for the officiating clergy.

quern A stone tool for grinding grain.

radiocarbon dating A scientific method of dating organic materials by measuring the quantity of radioactive carbon remaining in the sample; all living organisms absorb radioactive carbon from the atmosphere during life, and at death the carbon begins to decay at a known rate.

souterrain A subterranean trench lined with stones and roofed either with stones or with timber, for use as cool storage.

string-course A narrow horizontal band or course of stones projecting slightly from the face of a wall.

transept The north and south arms of a cruciform church.

tree-ring dating Also known as dendrochronology, this is a method of dating based on counting the annual growth rings of trees.

vallum A rampart and accompanying ditch, used here to denote a monastic enclosure.

Index

The author
Dr Anna Ritchie is a freelance archaeologist who has worked extensively in northern Britain. She is a Member of the Ancient Monuments Board for Scotland and a Trustee of the National Museums of Scotland. Her main areas of research are Neolithic Orkney and Early Historic Scotland. Her publications include *Prehistoric Orkney* and *Viking Scotland*, both in the Historic Scotland series.